NURSERY KNITS

NURSERY KNITS

TESSA WATTS-RUSSELL

HENRY HOLT AND COMPANY
NEW YORK

Publisher's Note
The patterns in this book are freely available for use by the private knitter, but may not be used on a commercial basis without the prior written permission of the Publisher.

Knitting Notes
Abbreviations: These are listed in the Knitting Know-how section on page 131.
Substituting different yarns: It is always advisable to use the yarn specified in the pattern. Yarn manufacturers' and agents' addresses are given on page 142. If, however, you find it necessary to substitute an alternative yarn, purchase only one ball at first and knit a large gauge swatch to make sure that the yarn is suitable for the pattern and produces results that are satisfactory.

The Designers
The majority of the designs in this book were created by Tessa Watts-Russell.
Additional material created by:
Rosanne Bartlett and Marjorie Moore of Blackberry Design (Christmas Trees, page 119; Pockets Top, page 50; Balloons, page 46)
Pearl Crook (Playtime, page 90)
Annabel Fox (Big Top, page 29)
Margaret Lambert of Sirdar Hand-knitting Yarns (Monday's Child, page 55; Sugar and Spice, page 21)
Debbie Scott for Patons (Bears in the Wood, page 100; Easter Chicks, page 10; Noël Noël, page 111; Lots of Dots, page 58).

Published in the United States by
Henry Holt and Company, Inc., 521 Fifth Avenue, New York, New York 10175.

Library of Congress Cataloging-in-Publication Data
Watts-Russell, Tessa.
    Nursery knits.

    1. Infants – Clothing.   2. Knitting – Patterns.
1. Title
TT825.W38   1987   746.43'2041   87– 217

ISBN-0-8050-0484-X

First American Edition
Printed in Hong Kong
10 9 8 7 6 5 4 3 2 1

0 - 8050 - 0484 - X

CONTENTS

SPRING FEVER

When spring is in the air, it means off with the old winter woolies and into lighter, cooler knitwear. Ducklings and bunnies are favorite spring themes, and they are here in abundance, along with Easter chicks, a frog, and a selection of interesting stitch patterns – some traditional, some new and all in fresh spring shades of lightweight to medium-weight yarns.

EASTER BUNNIES

Simple, yet adorable slipovers for child and teddy.

MEASUREMENTS
Child's slipover
To fit 18(20,22)" chest
Actual measurements 20(22,24)"
Length from shoulder 10(11,12)"
Teddy's slipover
To fit 15" chest

MATERIALS
Child's slipover
4(4,6) oz (100[100,150] g) of a lightweight smooth yarn, such as Pingouin Pingofine, in main color A
1 oz (20 g) of a lightweight angora-blend yarn in contrasting color B
Teddy's slipover
4 oz (100 g) of a lightweight smooth yarn in main color A
1 oz (20 g) of lightweight angora-blend yarn in contrasting color B
A pair each of size 0 and size 2 knitting needles
Stitch holder

GAUGE
32 sts and 40 rows to 4" measured over st st using smooth yarn and larger needles

To save time, take time to check gauge.

Real rabbits are soft to touch, and so are the fluffy white Easter bunnies on these gray slipovers. Because the bunnies are knitted in soft angora yarn, the sweaters should be washed by hand.

NOTE

Use contrasting color yarn B double throughout.

INSTRUCTIONS FOR CHILD'S SLIPOVER

BACK

⭐ Using smaller needles and A, cast on 81(89,97) sts.
Rib row 1: K1, ⭐ P1, K1, rep from ⭐ to end.
Rib row 2: K2, ⭐ P1, K1, rep from ⭐ to last st, K1.
Rep these 2 rows for 1(1,1½)", ending with rib row 2. ⭐
Change to larger needles.
Work in st st until back measures 4½(5½,6)" from beg, ending with a P row.
⭐⭐ **Shape armholes**
Next row: K4 sts and slip these sts onto a safety-pin, K to end.
Next row: P4 sts and slip these sts onto a safety-pin, P to end: 73(81,89) sts.
Next row: K2, K2 tog, K to last 4 sts, K2 tog tbl, K2.
Next row: P2, P2 tog tbl, P to last 4 sts, P2 tog, P2.
Rep the last 2 rows until 57(65,73) sts remain.
Next row: K2, K2 tog, K to last 4 sts, K2 tog tbl, K2.
Next row: P.
Rep these 2 rows until 49(57,65) sts remain, ending with a P row. ⭐⭐
Work straight until back measures 9½(10½,11½)" from beg.
End with a P row.
Shape neck
Next row: K6(10,14), K2 tog, K2, turn and leave remaining sts on a spare needle.
Dec 1 st at neck within the 2 st border until 6(10,14) sts remain.
Bind off.
Return to sts on spare needle. With right side facing, slip first 29 sts onto a holder, rejoin yarn and complete to match first side of neck, reversing all shaping.

FRONT

Work as for back from ⭐ to ⭐.
Change to larger needles.
Work in st st until front measures 22 rows less than back to armholes, ending with a P row.
Work motif from chart as follows:
Row 1: K22(26,30)A, 8B, 5A, 3B, 5A, 3B, 5A, 8B, 22(26,30)A.
Row 2: P22(26,30)A, 6B, 6A, 3B, 7A, 3B, 6A, 6B, 22(26,30)A.
Continue in this way, working from chart until row 22 has been completed.
Now work armhole shaping as for back from ⭐⭐ to ⭐⭐.
Shape neck
Next row: K14(18,22), K2 tog tbl, K2, turn and leave remaining sts on a spare needle.
Continue to dec 1 st within the 2 st border at neck edge on every row until 6(10,14) sts remain.
Work straight until front measures same as back to shoulder, ending with a P row. Bind off.
Return to sts on spare needle.
With right side facing, slip first 13 sts onto a holder, rejoin yarn and complete to match first side of neck, reversing all shaping.

NECKBAND

Join left shoulder seam.
With right side facing and using smaller needles and A, pick up and K4 sts down right back neck, K across 29 sts from back neck holder, pick up and K3 sts up left back neck and 36(36,40) sts down left front neck, K across 13 sts from front neck holder, then pick up and K36(36,40) sts up right front neck: 121(121,129) sts.
Beg with rib row 2, work 17 rows in rib as for back. Bind off.

ARMBANDS

Join right shoulder and neckband seam.
With right side facing and using smaller needles and A, pick up and K109(109,117) sts evenly around armhole including the 4 sts at each end on safety-pin.
Complete as for neckband.

TO FINISH

Block the work.
Join side and armband seams. Fold ribbing bands in half to wrong side and slipstitch in place.

INSTRUCTIONS FOR TEDDY'S SLIPOVER

BACK

⭐ Using smaller needles and A, cast on 67 sts.
Work 8 rows in rib as for child's slipover, inc 1 st at end of last row: 68 sts. ⭐
Change to larger needles.
Work in st st until back measures 3½" from beg, ending with a P row.

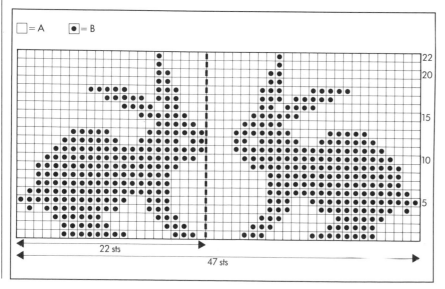

□ = A   ⦿ = B

22
20

15

10

5

22 sts

47 sts

Shape armholes

Next row: K4 sts and slip these sts onto a safety-pin, K to end.

Next row: P4 sts and slip these sts onto a safety-pin, P to end: 60 sts.

Dec 1 st each end of next 4 rows: 52 sts.

Work straight until back measures 6½" from beg, ending with a P row.

Shape neck

Next row: K10, K2 tog, turn and leave remaining sts on a spare needle.

Continue to dec 1 st at neck edge on every row until 8 sts remain. Now bind off.

Return to sts on spare needle.

With right side facing, slip first 28 sts onto a holder, rejoin yarn and complete to match first side of neck, reversing all shaping.

FRONT

Work as for back from ★ to ★.

Change to larger needles. Now work 2 rows st st.

Place single rabbit motif as indicated on chart as follows:

Row 1: K24A, 3B, 5A, 8B, 28A.

Row 2: P28A, 6B, 6A, 3B, 25A.

Continue in this way, working from chart until row 22 has been completed.

Shape neck

Next row: K20, turn and leave remaining sts on a spare needle.

Dec 1 st at neck edge on every row until 8 sts remain.

Work straight until front measures same as back to shoulders, ending with a P row.

Bind off.

Return to sts on spare needle.

With right side facing, slip first 12 sts onto a holder, rejoin yarn and complete to match first side of neck, reversing all shaping.

NECKBAND

Join left shoulder seam.

With right side facing and using smaller needles and A, pick up and K4 sts down right back neck, K across 28 sts from holder, pick up and K4 sts up left back neck and 33 sts down left front neck, K across 12 sts from holder, then pick up and K34 sts up right front neck: 115 sts.

Work 6 rows in rib as for child's slipover.

Bind off.

ARMBANDS

Join right shoulder and neckband seam.

With right side facing and using smaller needles and A, pick up and K85 sts evenly around armhole including the 4 sts at each end on safety-pins.

Complete as for neckband.

TO FINISH

Block the work.

Join side and armband seams.

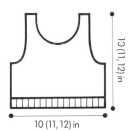

10 (11, 12) in

10 (11, 12) in

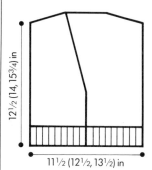

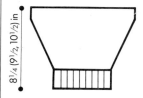

12½ (14, 15¾) in

11½ (12½, 13½) in

8¼ (9½, 10½) in

EASTER CHICKS

A simple cardigan covered with Easter chicks.

MEASUREMENTS
To fit 18(20,22)" chest
Actual measurements 23(25,27)"
Length from shoulder 12½(14,15¾)"
Sleeve seam 8¼(9½,10½)"

MATERIALS
6(6,8) oz (150[150,200]g) of a lightweight smooth yarn, such as Pingouin Pingofine, in main color A
2(2,4) oz (50[50,100]g) of same in contrasting color B
2 oz (50 g) of same in contrasting color C
3 buttons
A pair each of size 2 and size 3 knitting needles and one size 2 circular needle, any length
Stitch holder

GAUGE
28 sts and 32 rows to 4" measured over st st worked on size 3 needles

To save time, take time to check gauge.

INSTRUCTIONS

BACK
Using smaller needles and A, cast on 82(90,98) sts.
Rib row 1: K2, * P2, K2, rep from * to end.
Rib row 2: P2, * K2, P2, rep from * to end.
Rep these 2 rows once more.
Change to B and work 2 rows rib, then change back

to A and continue in rib until work measures 2", ending with rib row 2. Change to larger needles. Proceed in st st, working in pat from chart and repeating pat as necessary until work measures 12½(14,15¾)" from beg, ending with a P row.
Shape shoulders
Bind off 13(14,16) sts at beg of next 2 rows and 13(15,16) sts at beg of following 2 rows. Cut off yarn and leave remaining 30(32,34) sts on a holder.

LEFT FRONT
Using smaller needles and A, cast on 38(42,46) sts and work in rib as for back for 4 rows.
Change to B and work 2 rows rib, then change back to A and continue in rib until work measures 2". Change to larger needles. Proceed in st st, working in pat from chart as indicated until work measures 5½(6¼,7)", ending with a K row.
Shape neck
Keeping pat correct, dec 1 st at beg of next and every following 4th row until 26(29,32) sts remain. Work straight until front measures same as back to shoulder, ending at armhole edge.
Shape shoulder
Bind off 13(14,16) sts at beg of next row. Work one row straight. Bind off 13(15,16) sts at beg of next row.

RIGHT FRONT
Work as for left front, reversing all shaping and working from chart as indicated for right front.

SLEEVES
Using smaller needles and A, cast on 42(46,50) sts.
Work in rib as for back for 4 rows.
Change to B and work 2 rows in rib. Change back to A and continue in rib until work measures 2".

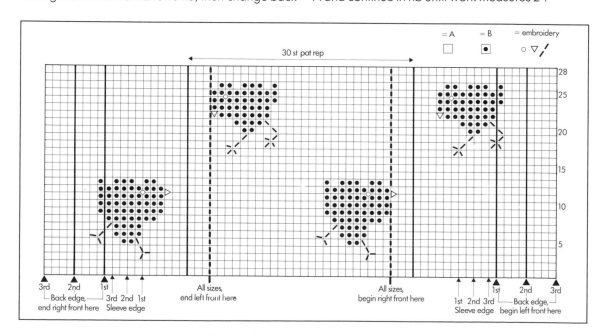

Springtime wouldn't be spring without baby chicks, and this classic V-neck cardigan is covered with them! They are knitted in while the cardigan is made – although they could instead be duplicate-stitched on afterward.

Change to larger needles.
Continue in st st, working in pat from chart as indicated for sleeve and AT THE SAME TIME inc and work into pat 1 st each end of 3rd and every following 3rd(4th,4th) row until there are 76(80,84) sts.
Work straight until sleeve measures 8¼(9½,10½)", ending with a P row.
Bind off.

BUTTON AND BUTTONHOLE BORDER

Press or block, as appropriate for yarn used.
Join shoulder seams.
With right side facing and using the circular needle, pick up and K44(51,56) sts up right front to beg of neck shaping and 56(64,72) sts up right front neck to shoulder seam, K across 30(32,34) sts from back neck holder, then pick up and K56(64,72) sts down left front neck to beg of neck shaping and 44(51,56) sts down left front to cast-on edge: 230(262, 290) sts.
Beg with rib row 2, work 3 rows rib as for back, ending with right side facing.
Buttonhole row: Rib 6, [bind off 3, rib 14(17,20) sts] twice, bind off 3, rib to end.
Next row: Rib to end, casting on 3 sts over those bound off.
Change to B and work 2 rows rib, then change back to A and work 2 rows rib.
Using A, bind off in rib.

TO FINISH

Using C, embroider beaks and feet on chicks.
Placing center of tops of sleeves at shoulder seams, sew in sleeves. Join side and sleeve seams. Sew on buttons opposite buttonholes.

OH DUCKY!

This pretty little woolen pinafore has a sitting duck on its cross-over front.

MEASUREMENTS
To fit 18–20(20–22)" chest
Length from shoulder 17(19)"

MATERIALS
6 oz (150 g) of a lightweight smooth yarn, such as Anny Blatt Baby' Blatt, in main color A
2 oz (50 g) of same in contrasting colors B and C
A pair each of size 2 and size 3 knitting needles

GAUGE
28 sts and 38 rows to 4" measured over st st worked on size 3 needles

To save time, take time to check gauge.

INSTRUCTIONS

BACK
⋆ Using larger needles and B, cast on 140(164) sts.
K 1 row.
Change to C and K 2 rows.
Change to B and K 2 rows.
Rep these 4 rows 4 more times.
Break off B and C.
Change to A.
Working in A only, continue in st st until work measures 9½(10½)" from beg, ending with a K row.
Next row: (wrong side) K1, P1 ⋆ P2 tog, rep from ⋆ to last 2 sts, P1, K1: 72(84) sts.

Waistband
Change to smaller needles.
Working in stripes of 2 rows B, 2 rows C, K 22 rows. ⋆
Using B, bind off.

FRONT
Work as for back from ⋆ to ⋆, but do not bind off.

Left front bib
Next row: Using B, bind off 8(12) sts changing to A for the last st, change to larger needles, then K until there are 40(42) sts on the needle, turn and leave remaining 24(30) sts on a spare needle.
Break off B.
Work in A.
Next row: K5, P to last 5 sts, K5.
Next row: K.
Next row: K5, P to last 5 sts, K5.
Work motif from chart.
Shape bib as follows:
Next row: K12A, 6B, 15(17)A, with A K2 tog, K5.
Next row: K5A, P13(15)A, 11B, 5A, K5A.
Keeping 5 st g st border on each edge and dec 1 st at neck edge within border as before on next and every other row, continue to work from chart until row 16 has been completed.
Now continue to dec at neck edge as before until 16(18) sts remain.
Work straight until work measures 12(14)" from top of waistband, ending with a wrong-side row.
Bind off.

Right front bib
With right side facing and using larger needles and A, pick up and K the back loops of the last 24 sts from behind the left front bib, K across the first 16(18) sts from spare needle, then changing to a smaller needle and a separate length of B, bind off the final 8(12) sts.
Continuing on these 40(42) sts and using A, complete to match left front bib, omitting motif and working K2 tog tbl when decreasing.

TO FINISH
Press or block, as appropriate for yarn used.
Join side seams of skirt. Sew ends of straps to waistband at back.

 This lightweight knitted pinafore is ideal for those bright spring days that are too warm for winter knits but not yet warm enough for cotton. The pinafore has bands of garter stitch at the hem and high waist and a little duck motif on the cross-over front.

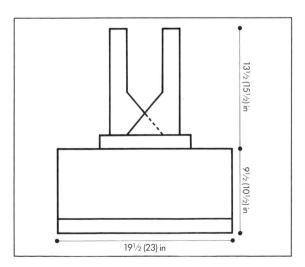

13½ (15½) in
9½ (10½) in
19½ (23) in

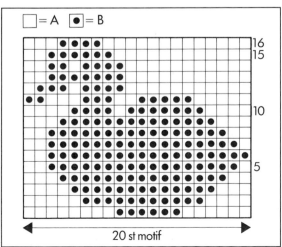

☐ = A   ⚫ = B

16
15

10

5

20 st motif

A thick, textured sweater in 4 ply yarn that is ideal for those breezy spring days when there is still a sharp chill in the air.

SPRING CABLE

An unusual raglan-sleeved pullover.

MEASUREMENTS
To fit 18–20(20–22)" chest
Actual measurements 24(26)"
Length from shoulder 12¾(14¾)"
Sleeve seam 8(9)"

MATERIALS
8 oz (200 g) of a lightweight smooth yarn, such as Anny Blatt Baby' Blatt
A pair each of size 2 and size 4 knitting needles
Cable needle and 3 stitch holders

GAUGE
26 sts and 36 rows to 4" measured over pat worked on size 4 needles

To save time, take time to check gauge.

SPECIAL ABBREVIATIONS
C4, Cable 4 as follows: slip next 2 sts onto cable needle and hold at back of work, K2, then K2 from cable needle.
C3B, Cable 3 back as follows: slip next 2 sts onto cable needle and hold at back of work, K1, then K2 from cable needle.
C3F, Cable 3 front as follows: slip next st onto cable needle and hold at front of work, K2, then K1 from cable needle.
C6, Cable 6 as follows: slip next 3 sts onto cable needle and hold at back of work, K3, then K3 from cable needle.

INSTRUCTIONS

BACK
★ Using smaller needles cast on 80(86) sts.
Beg waistband pat as follows:
Row 1: K1, P1, ★ K4, P2, rep from ★ to last 6 sts, K4, P1, K1.
Row 2 and every other row: K2, ★ P4, K2, rep from ★ to end.
Row 3: K1, P1, ★ K4, P2, rep from ★ to last 6 sts, K4, P1, K1.
Row 5: K1, P1, ★ C4, P2, rep from ★ to last 6 sts, C4, P1, K1.
Rows 7 to 18: Rep rows 3 to 6 three times.
Row 19: P. ★
Row 20: Inc in first st, P to last st, K1: 81(87) sts.
Change to larger needles.
Work in pat as follows:
Row 1: K.
Row 2: K1, P to last st, K1.
Row 3: K2, ★ P2, K1, rep from ★ to last st, K1.

Row 4: As row 2.
These 4 rows form the pat.
Continue in pat until back measures 6(7)" from beg, ending with a 4th pat row.
Shape raglan
Bind off 4 sts at beg of next 2 rows: 73(79) sts.
Work 4 rows straight in pat.
Next row: K1, K2 tog tbl, pat to last 3 sts, K2 tog, K1.
Work 3 rows straight.
Rep the last 4 rows until 67(73) sts remain, then dec on every other row until 57 sts remain, ending with a wrong-side row.
Divide for back opening
Next row: K1, K2 tog tbl, pat across 23 sts, K3, turn and leave remaining sts on a spare needle.
Next row: K3, pat to end.
Continuing to work 3 sts in g st at neck edge, dec 1 st as before at raglan edge on next and every other row until 22 sts remain.
Next row (buttonhole row): K1, K2 tog tbl, pat 16, yo, K2 tog, K1.
Next row: K3, pat to end.
Now continue dec as before until 17 sts remain.
Break off yarn and leave sts on a holder.
Return to remaining sts.
With right side facing, join yarn to first st and cast on 4 sts, pat to last 3 sts, K2 tog, K1: 32 sts.
Next row: Pat to last 4 sts, K4.
Continuing to work 4 sts in g st at neck edge, dec 1 st as before at raglan edge on next and every other row until 20 sts remain.
Break off yarn and leave sts on holder.

FRONT
Work as for back from ★ to ★.
Next row: K1, P to last st, K1: 80(86) sts.
Change to larger needles.
Work in pat with central cable panel as follows:
Row 1: K26(29), P2, K7, P2, K6, P2, K7, P2, K26(29).
Row 2: K1, P25(28), K2, P7, K2, P6, K2, P7, K2, P25(28), K1.
Row 3: K2, [P2, K1] 8(9) times, P2, C3B, K1, C3F, P2, C6, P2, C3B, K1, C3F, P2, [K1, P2] 8(9) times, K2.
Row 4: As row 2.
These 4 rows form pat.
Continue in pat until front measures same as back to beg of raglan shaping, ending with a 4th pat row.
Shape raglan
Bind off 4 sts at beg of next 2 rows: 72(78) sts.
Work 4 rows straight in pat.
Next row: K1, K2 tog tbl, pat to last 3 sts, K2 tog, K1.
Work 3 rows straight.
Rep the last 4 rows until 66(72) sts remain, then dec on every other row until 52 sts remain, ending with a wrong-side row.
Divide for neck
Next row: K1, K2 tog tbl, pat 13, K2 tog, turn and leave remaining sts on a spare needle.

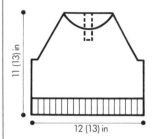

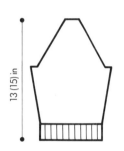

Continuing to dec at raglan edge as before, dec 1 st at neck edge on every row until 9 sts remain. Keeping neck edge straight, continue to dec at raglan edge only until 2 sts remain, ending with a wrong-side row.
Bind off.
Return to remaining sts.
With right side facing, sl first 16 sts onto a holder, join yarn to next st, K2 tog, pat to last 3 sts, K2 tog, K1.
Now complete 2nd side of neck to match first side, reversing all shaping.

SLEEVES

Using smaller needles cast on 44 sts.
Work rows 1 to 19 as for waistband pat on back.
Next row: Inc in first st, P to last st, K1: 45 sts.
Change to larger needles.
Working in pat as for back, inc and work into pat 1 st each end of 7th and every following 6th row until there are 57(63) sts.
Work straight until sleeve measures 8(9)" from beg, ending with a 4th pat row.
Shape raglan
Bind off 4 sts at beg of next 2 rows: 49(55) sts.
Work 4 rows straight in pat.
Next row: K1, K2 tog tbl, pat to last 3 sts, K2 tog, K1.
Work 3 rows straight.
Rep the last 4 rows until 43(49) sts remain, then dec on every other row until 9 sts remain, ending with a wrong-side row.
Break off yarn and leave remaining sts on a holder.

NECKBAND

With right side facing and using smaller needles, K20 sts from left back neck holder and 9 sts from top of one sleeve, pick up and K20 sts down left side of front neck. K across 16 sts from front neck holder, pick up and K20 sts up right side of front neck, then K across 9 sts from second sleeve and 17 sts from right back neck holder: 111 sts.
Next row: P.
Now continue in pat as follows:
Row 1: K4, ✳ P2, K4, rep from ✳ to last 5 sts, P2, K3.
Row 2: K5, ✳ P4, K2, rep from ✳ to last 4 sts, K4.
Row 3: K4, ✳ P2, C4, rep from ✳ to last 5 sts, P2, yo, K2 tog, K1.
Row 4: As row 2.
Row 5: As row 1.
Row 6: As row 2.
Row 7: As row 3 to last 5 sts, then P2, K3.
Row 8: As row 2.
Bind off.

TO FINISH

Block if necessary, but do not press.
Join raglan seams. Sew lower edge of button border in place behind buttonhole border. Sew on buttons.
Join side and sleeve seams.

LAURIE LAMBKIN

An adorable wooly lamb, just like the real thing!

MEASUREMENT
Height approximately 13"

MATERIALS
6 oz (150 g) of a bouclé yarn
Small amounts of smooth lightweight yarn for ear linings
Black and blue for embroidering eyes
Polyester stuffing
A pair each of size 3 and size 5 knitting needles

GAUGE
18 sts and 32 rows to 4" measured over g st worked on size 5 needles

To save time, take time to check gauge.

NOTE
The legs, body, head and ears are all worked in garter st using bouclé yarn.

INSTRUCTIONS

LEFT FRONT LEG
✱✱ Using larger needles and bouclé yarn, cast on 10 sts.
K 34 rows.
Next row: Inc in first st, K to end.
Next row: K to last st, inc in last st.
Rep these 2 rows until there are 18 sts.
Break off yarn and leave sts on a spare needle.

LEFT BACK LEG
Using larger needles and bouclé yarn, cast on 10 sts.
K 24 rows.
Shape leg
Row 1: K to last st, inc in last st: 11 sts.
Row 2: K.
Rows 3 and 4: As rows 1 and 2: 12 sts.
Row 5: K2 tog, K to last st, inc in last st: 12 sts.
Row 6: K.
Rep rows 5 and 6 seven more times.
Join legs
K across 12 sts of back leg, then K across 18 sts of front leg: 30 sts. ✱
K 19 rows.
Shape back
Row 1: K2 tog, K to end.
Row 2: K to last 2 sts, K2 tog.
Rep these 2 rows until 24 sts remain.
Head
Row 1: Bind off 14 sts, K to last st, inc in last st: 11 sts.
Row 2: Inc in first st, K to last st, inc in last st: 13 sts.

Rows 3 to 7: Rep row 2 five times: 23 sts.
Row 8: K.
Row 9: [K5, inc in next st] 3 times, K5: 26 sts.
Rows 10 to 12: K.
Row 13: K to last 2 sts, K2 tog: 25 sts.
Row 14: K.
Rows 15 to 20: Rep rows 13 and 14 three times:
22 sts.
Dec 1 st each end of next and every other row: 18 sts.
Dec 1 st each end of every row until 8 sts remain.
Next row: K1, [skpo] 3 times, K1: 5 sts. Bind off. ★★

RIGHT FRONT, BACK LEGS, BODY AND HEAD
Work as for left side from ★★ to ★★.

INSIDE LEG GUSSET (make 2)
Work as for left front and back legs from ★★ to ★.
K 9 rows. Bind off.

EARS (make 2)
Using larger needles and bouclé yarn cast on 12 sts.
K 22 rows.
Shape top
Dec 1 st each end of next and every other row until
4 sts remain. Now K 1 row.

Next row: [K2 tog] twice: 2 sts. Now K 1 row.
Change to smaller needles and smooth yarn and
work ear lining as follows:
Row 1: Inc into each st: 4 sts.
Row 2: P.
Row 3: Inc into each st: 8 sts.
Row 4: P.
Continuing in st st, inc 1 st each end of next and
every other row until there are 20 sts.
Work straight until lining measures the same length
as outer ear, ending with a wrong-side row. Bind off.

TAIL
Using larger needles and bouclé yarn, cast on 28 sts.
Work 8 rows rev st st. Bind off.

TO FINISH
Join side seams on ears. Join leg gussets to legs and
body, joining seam at top of gusset. Join seam
around head and down center back leaving a small
opening at back of head for stuffing. Turn right side
out and stuff firmly, then close opening neatly. Fold
ears in half at base and sew in place at sides of
head. Embroider eyes and nose as shown in picture.
Join seam on tail and sew in place.

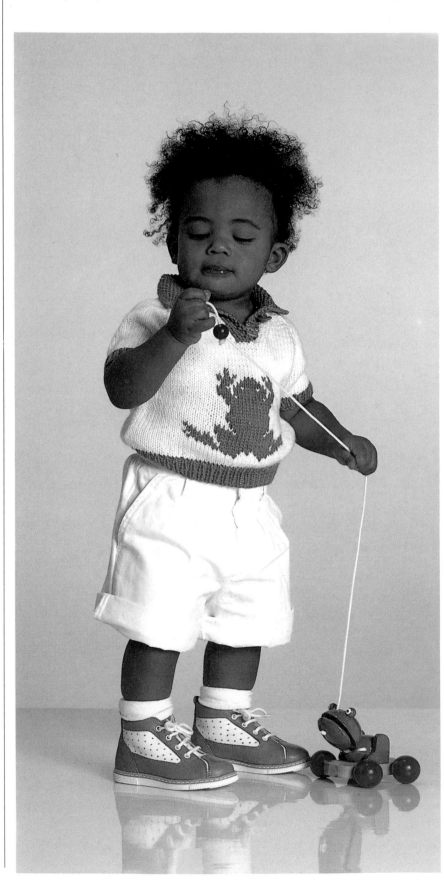

FREDDY FROG

A practical cotton-mix top with a clever frog motif.

MEASUREMENTS
To fit 18(20,22)" chest
Actual measurements 21(23,25)"
Length from shoulder 11(12,13)"
Sleeve seam 2½(3,4)"

MATERIALS
6(8,8) oz (150[200,200] g) of a smooth cotton or
cotton-acrylic yarn, such as Phildar Satine No 4, in
main color A
2(4,4) oz (50[100,100] g) of same in contrasting
color B
A pair each of size 3 and size 5 knitting needles
2 buttons and a stitch holder

GAUGE
22 sts and 28 rows to 4" measured over st st worked
on size 5 needles

To save time, take time to check gauge.

INSTRUCTIONS

BACK
★ Using smaller needles and B, cast on 55(61,67) sts.
Rib row 1: K2, ★ Pl, K1, rep from ★ to last st, K1.
Rib row 2: K1, ★ P1, K1, rep from ★ to end.
Rep these 2 rows 4 more times.
Change to larger needles.
Break off B.
Join in A.
Inc row: K10(14,16), ★ inc in next st, K10, rep from ★ to
last 12(14,18) sts, inc in next st, K to end: 59(65,71) sts. ★
Beg P row, work in st st until back measures
6(6½,7½)" from beg, ending with a P row.
Shape raglans
Bind off 3(3,4) sts at beg of next 2 rows:
53(59,63) sts. Work 2 rows st st.
Next row: K1, K2 tog tbl, K to last 3 sts, K2 tog, K1.
Next row: P.
Rep these 2 rows until 21(23,27) sts remain, ending
with a P row.
Break off yarn and leave remaining sts on a holder.

SLEEVES
Using smaller needles and B, cast on 41(45,47) sts.
Work 6 rows in rib as for back.
Change to larger needles. Break off B. Join in A.
Inc row: K8(9,10), ★ inc in next st, K7(8,9), rep from ★
to last 9(9,10) sts, inc in next st, K to end:
45(49,51) sts.
Beg with a P row, work in st st until sleeve measures
2½(3,4)" from beg, ending with a P row.

Shape raglan

Bind off 3(3,4) sts at beg of next 2 rows:
39(43,43) sts. Work 2 rows st st.
Next row: K1, K2 tog tbl, K to last 3 sts, K2 tog, K1.
Next row: P
Rep these 2 rows until 7 sts remain, ending with a P row.
Break off yarn and leave sts on a holder.

FRONT

Work as for back from ★ to ★.
Beg with a P row, work 3 rows st st.
Now work frog motif from chart as follows:
Row 1: K26(29,32)A, 1B, 5A, 1B, 26(29,32)A.
Row 2: P24(27,30)A, 3B, 5A, 3B, 24(27,30)A.
Continue in pat from chart until row 30 has been completed.
Continue in A only until front measures same as back to beg of raglan shaping, ending with a P row.

Shape raglans

Work raglan shaping as for back until 49(55,59) sts remain, ending with a P row.

Divide for neck

Next row: K1, K2 tog tbl, K19(22,24), turn and leave remaining sts on a spare needle.
Next row: Join in B and cast on 5 sts for button band; over these 5 sts work [K1, P1] twice, K1, change to A and P to end.
★★ Always twisting A and B together when changing color to avoid making a hole, keep 5 st border worked in seed st and B as set and AT THE SAME TIME continue raglan shaping as before in A until 17(20,22) sts remain, ending with a wrong-side row. ★★

Shape neck

Next row: K1, K2 tog tbl, K4(6,6), K2 tog, K1, turn and leave remaining sts on a safety-pin.
Next row: P1, P2 tog, P to end.
Next row: K1, K2 tog tbl, K to last 3 sts, K2 tog, K1.
Next row: P1, P2 tog, P to end: 4(5,5) sts.
Now continue to dec at raglan edge only as before until 2 sts remain.
Bind off.
Return to sts on spare needle.
With right side facing, join B to first st and K5, join in A then K to last 3 sts, K2 tog, K1.
Continuing to dec at raglan edge on every other row as before and working 5 st border in seed st and B, work as for first side of neck from ★★ to ★★, working buttonhole on the 7th row as follows:
Buttonhole row (right side): K1, P1, yo, sl 1, K1, psso, K1, change to A and K to last 3 sts, K2 tog, K1.

Shape neck

Do not cut off B. Slip first 7(8,10) sts onto a safety-pin. Using A only K1, K2 tog tbl, K to last 3 sts, K2 tog, K1.
Dec 1 st at neck edge on next 2 rows and AT THE SAME TIME continue to dec at raglan edge as before until 2 sts remain. Bind off.

COLLAR

With right side facing and using larger needles and yarn from right front border at neck edge, work across sts on safety-pin as follows: K1, P1, yo, sl 1, K1, psso, K3(4,6), pick up and K9(11,11) sts up right side of front neck, K across 7 sts from top of right sleeve, 21(23,27) sts across back neck and 7 sts across top of left sleeve, pick up and K9(11,11) sts down left side of front neck, K the first 3(4,6) sts from safety-pin, then (P1, K1) twice: 67(75,83) sts.
Work 2 rows in seed st. Continuing in seed st, bind off 2 sts at beg of next 2 rows.
Work another 16 rows seed st. Bind off.

TO FINISH

Press or block, as appropriate for yarn used.
Join raglan seams, then join side and sleeve seams. Catch button border in place at base of buttonhole border. Sew on buttons.

This practical short-sleeved raglan top is ideal for mischievous rascals of the "snips and snails and puppy dogs' tails" variety!

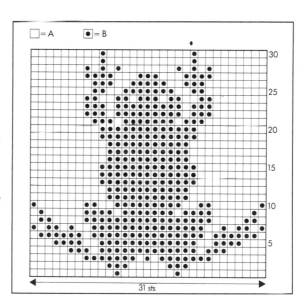

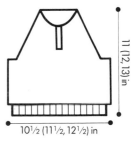

11 (12,13) in

10½ (11½, 12½) in

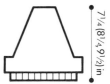

7¼ (8¼, 9½) in

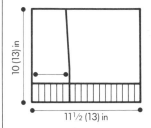

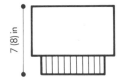

10 (13) in

11½ (13) in

7 (8) in

SUGAR AND SPICE

A charming pullover and matching cardigan.

MEASUREMENTS
To fit 22(24)" chest
Actual measurements:
Cardigan
Length from shoulder 10(12)"
Pullover
Length from shoulder 9¼(11¾)"

MATERIALS
Cardigan
2(3) oz 40[80] g) of a fine smooth yarn, such as
Sirdar Snuggly 2 ply
4 buttons
Pullover
2(3) oz (0[0] g) of same
A pair each of size 2 and size 3 knitting needles
A size B crochet hook
2 buttons and 3 stitch holders

GAUGE
2 pattern repeats (20 sts) and 25 rows measure 2⅜"
over pattern using size 3 needles.

To save time, take time to check gauge.

INSTRUCTIONS FOR CARDIGAN

BACK
Using smaller needles cast on 93(103) sts.
Rib row 1: Sl 1, K1, ✶ P1, K1, rep from ✶ to last st, K1.
Rib row 2: Sl 1, ✶ P1, K1, rep from ✶ to end.
Rep these 2 rows 10 more times.
Change to larger needles. Work in pat as follows:
Row 1: Sl 1, K1, ✶ yo, skpo, K2 tog, yo, K1, rep from ✶
to last st, K1.
Row 2 and every other row: Sl 1, P to last st, K1.
Row 3: Sl 1, K2, ✶ yo, skpo, K3, K2 tog, yo, K3, rep
from ✶ to end.
Row 5: Sl 1, K3 ✶ yo, skpo, K1, K2 tog, yo, K5, rep
from ✶ to last 9 sts, yo, skpo, K1, K2 tog, yo, K4.
Row 7: Sl 1, K4 ✶ yo, sl 1, K2 tog, psso, yo, K7, rep
from ✶ to last 8 sts, yo, sl 1, K2 tog, psso, yo, K5.
Row 9: Sl 1, K1, ✶ skpo, K2, yo, K1, yo, K2, K2 tog,
K1, rep from ✶ to last st, K1.
Row 11: As row 9.
Row 13: As row 9.
Row 14: Sl 1, P to last st, K1.
These 14 rows form the pat.
Continue in pat until work measures 10(13)" from
beg, ending with a wrong-side row.
Shape shoulders
Bind off 30(34) sts in pat at beg of next 2 rows.
Bind off remaining 33 sts in pat.

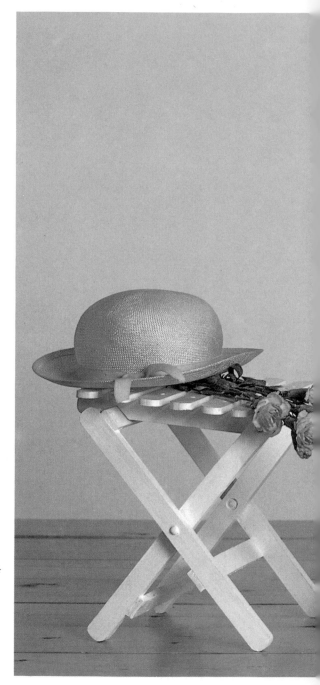

LEFT FRONT
★ Using smaller needles cast on 33(43) sts.
Work 22 rows in rib as for back. ★
Change to larger needles.
Work rows 1 to 14 of pat as for back.
Shape front edge
Keeping pat correct, dec 1 st at end of next and
every following 24th(40th) row until 30(34) sts
remain.
Work straight until front measures same as back,
ending with a wrong-side row. Bind off in pat.

"What are little girls made of?
What are little girls made of?
Sugar and spice and
*   everything nice,*
That's what little girls are
*   made of!"*

RIGHT FRONT

Work as for left front from ⋆ to ⋆.
Change to larger needles.
Work rows 1 to 14 of pat as for back.

Shape front edge

Keeping pat correct, dec 1 st at beg of next and every following 24th(40th) row until 30(34) sts remain.
Work straight until front measures same as back, ending with a right-side row.
Bind off purlwise.

SLEEVES

Using smaller needles cast on 51(55) sts.
Rib row 1: Sl 1, K1, ⋆ P1, K1, rep from ⋆ to last st, K1.
Rib row 2: Sl 1, ⋆ P1, K1, rep from ⋆ to end.
Rep these 2 rows 9 more times, then rib row 1 again.
Inc row: Sl 1, rib 1(3), ⋆ inc in next st, P1, rep from ⋆ to last 3 sts, rib to end: 73(83) sts.
Change to larger needles.
Work in pat as for back until sleeve measures 7(8)" from beg, ending with a wrong-side row.
Bind off in pat.

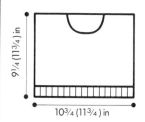

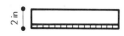

9¼ (11¾) in

10¾ (11¾) in

2 in

RIGHT FRONT BORDER
Join shoulder seams.
Using smaller needles cast on 35 sts.
Row 1: Sl 1, K1, * P1, K1, rep from * to last st, K1.
Row 2: Sl 1, * P1, K1, rep from * to end.
Rep these 2 rows once more.
Row 5: Sl 1, [K1, P1] twice, K1, bind off 2 sts, [K1, P1] 9 times, bind off 2 sts, [P1, K1] twice, K1.
Row 6: Sl 1, [P1, K1] twice, P1, cast on 2 sts, [K1, P1] 9 times, K1, cast on 2 sts, [P1, K1] 3 times.
Rows 7 to 16: Rep rows 1 and 2 five times.
Rows 17 and 18: Rep rows 5 and 6 once.
Rows 19 to 22: Rep rows 1 and 2 twice.
Row 23: Bind off 20 sts in rib, [K1, P1] 6 times, K2: 15 sts.
Row 24: Sl 1, * P1, K1, rep from * to end.
Continue in rib, dec 1 st at end of the 43rd row from beg and every following 16th row until 11 sts remain.
Work straight until border is long enough to go up front and around to center back neck, ending with a wrong-side row.
Bind off in rib.

LEFT FRONT BORDER
Using smaller needles cast on 35 sts.
Row 1: Sl 1, K1, * P1, K1, rep from * to last st, K1.
Row 2: Sl 1, * P1, K1, rep from * to end.
Rep these 2 rows 10 more times.
Row 23: Sl 1, [K1, P1] 7 times, bind off remaining 20 sts in rib, then fasten off.
Row 24: With wrong side facing, rejoin yarn to remaining 15 sts, K1, [P1, K1] 7 times.
Continue in rib, dec 1 st at beg of the 43rd row from beg and every following 16th row until 11 sts remain.
Work straight until border is long enough to go up front and around to center back neck, ending with a wrong-side row.
Bind off in rib.

TO FINISH
Block the work.
Placing center of tops of sleeves at shoulder seams, sew in sleeves.
Join side and sleeve seams.
Join ends of borders, then placing seam at center back neck, sew front borders in place. Sew on buttons opposite buttonholes.

INSTRUCTIONS FOR PULLOVER

BACK
** Using smaller needles cast on 89(99) sts.
Rib row 1: Sl 1, K1, * P1, K1, rep from * to last st, K1.
Rib row 2: Sl 1, * P1, K1, rep from * to end.
Rep these 2 rows 6 more times.
Change to larger needles.
Work in pat as follows:
Row 1: Sl 1, K1, K2 tog, yo, K1, * yo, skpo, K2 tog, yo, K1, rep from * to last 4 sts, yo, skpo, K2.
Row 2 and every other row: Sl 1, P to last st, K1.
Row 3: Sl 1, * yo, skpo, K3, K2 tog, yo, K3, rep from * to last 8 sts, yo, skpo, K3, K2 tog, yo, K1.
Row 5: Sl 1, K1, * yo, skpo, K1, K2 tog, yo, K5, rep from * to last 7 sts, yo, skpo, K1, K2 tog, yo, K2.
Row 7: Sl 1, K2, * yo, sl 1, K2 tog, psso, yo, K7, rep from * to last 6 sts, yo, sl 1, K2 tog, psso, yo, K3.
Row 9: Sl 1, K4, yo, K2, K2 tog, K1, * skpo, K2, yo, K1, yo, K2, K2 tog, K1, rep from * to last 9 sts, skpo, K2, yo, K5.
Row 11: As row 9.
Row 13: As row 9.
Row 14: Sl 1, P to last st, K1.
These 14 rows form the pat. **
Continue in pat until work measures 6(9)″ from beg, ending with a wrong-side row.
Divide for back opening
Next row: Sl 1, pat 43(48) sts, K2 tog, pat 42(47) sts, K1.
Next row: Sl 1, pat 42(47) sts, K1, turn and leave remaining sts on a spare needle.
Work straight until back measures 9¼(11¾)″ from beg.
Ending with a right-side row.
Shape shoulder
Next row: Bind off 28(33) sts purlwise, P to last st, K1.
Break off yarn and leave remaining 16 sts on a holder.
With wrong side facing, rejoin yarn to remaining sts and work as follows:
Next row: Sl 1, pat to last st, K1.
Work straight until back measures 9¼(11¾)″ from beg, ending with a wrong-side row.
Shape shoulder
Next row: Bind off 28(33) sts in pat, pat to last st, K1.
Next row: Sl 1, P to last st, K1.
Break off yarn and leave remaining 16 sts on a holder.

FRONT
Work as for back from ★★ to ★★.
Continue in pat until work measures 7¼(9¾)" from beg, ending with a wrong-side row.
Shape neck
Next row: Sl 1, pat 35(40) sts, turn and leave remaining sts on a spare needle.
Next row: Sl 1, P to last st, K1.
Dec 1 st at neck edge on next 8 rows: 28(33) sts.
Work straight until front measures same as back, ending with a wrong-side row.
Bind off in pat.
Return to remaining sts.
With right side facing, slip first 17 sts onto a holder, and rejoin yarn to remaining sts.
Work as follows:
Next row: K1, pat to last st, K1.
Next row: Sl 1, P to last st, K1.
Dec 1 st at neck edge on next 8 rows: 28(33) sts.
Work straight until front measures same as back, ending with a right-side row.
Bind off purlwise.

SLEEVES
Using smaller needles cast on 79 sts.
Rib row 1: Sl 1, K1, ★ P1, K1, rep from ★ to last st, K1.
Rib row 2: Sl 1, ★ P1, K1, rep from ★ to end.
Rep these 2 rows twice more.
Change to larger needles.
Work rows 1 to 14 as for back.
Bind off in pat.

NECKBAND
Block the work.
Join shoulder seams.
With right side facing, using smaller needles and beg at left side of back neck, K across 16 sts on holder at back neck, pick up and K15 sts evenly down left side of front neck, K across 17 sts on front neck holder, pick up and K15 sts evenly up right side of front neck, then K across 16 sts from holder at right side of back neck: 79 sts.
Rib row 1: Sl 1, ★ P1, K1, rep from ★ to end.
Rib row 2: Sl 1, K1, ★ P1, K1, rep from ★ to last st, K1.
Rep these 2 rows twice more.
Now work rib row 1 again.
Bind off in rib.

BUTTONHOLE BORDER
With right side facing, using a size B crochet hook and beg at top of right back opening, work 24 sc evenly down back opening, turn.
Row 1: Ch 1 (to count as first sc), 1 sc into each of next 8 sc, ch 2, skip 2 sc, 1 sc into each of next 8 sc, ch 2, skip 2 sc, 1 sc into each of next 3 sc, turn.
Row 2: Ch 1, 1 sc into each of next 2 sc, 2 sc into 2 ch sp, 1 sc into each of next 8 sc, 2 sc into 2 ch sp, 1 sc into each of next 9 sc. Fasten off.

BUTTON BORDER
With right side facing, using a size B crochet hook and beg at lower edge of left back opening, work 24 sc evenly up back opening, turn.
Work 2 rows in sc. Fasten off.

TO FINISH
Placing center of tops of sleeves at shoulder seams, sew in sleeves. Join side and sleeve seams. Lap buttonhole border over button border and sew in place at lower edge.
Sew on buttons opposite buttonholes.

The classic combination of pullover and cardigan is especially pretty when made in a delicate lacy stitch like this one and is ideal for mild spring weather. See stitch sample opposite.

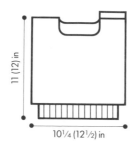

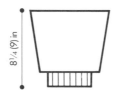

11 (12) in

10¼ (12½) in

8¼ (9) in

BASKET WEAVE

A round neck pullover with a woven effect.

MEASUREMENTS
To fit 18–20(20–22)" chest
Actual measurements 20½(25)"
Length from shoulders 11(12)"
Sleeve seam 8¼(9)"

MATERIALS
6(8) oz (150[200] g) of a lightwight smooth yarn, such as Phildar Luxe
A pair each of size 1 and size 2 knitting needles
4 buttons and 2 stitch holders

GAUGE
36 sts and 48 rows to 4" measured over pat

To save time, take time to check gauge.

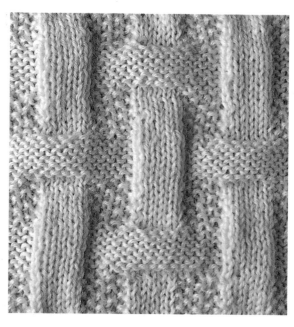

INSTRUCTIONS

BACK
Using smaller needles cast on 94(114)sts.
Rib row 1: K2, * P2, K2, rep from * to end.
Rib row 2: K1, P1, * K2, P2, rep from * to last 4 sts, K2, Pl, K1.
Rep these 2 rows for 1½", ending with rib row 1.
Inc row: Rib 16(24), * inc in next st, rib 15, rep from * to last 14(26)sts, inc in next st, rib to end: 99(119) sts.
Change to larger needles.
Proceed in pat as follows:
Row 1: K2, * [K1, P1] twice, K6, rep from * to last 7 sts, [K1, P1] twice, K3.

Row 2: K1, P1, * [K1, P1] twice, K1, P5, ref from * to last 7 sts, [K1, P1] twice, K1, P1, K1.
Rows 3 to 8: Rep rows 1 and 2 three times.
Row 9: K2, P15(5), * K5, P15, rep from * to last 22(12) sts, K5, P15(5), K2.
Row 10: K1, P1, K15(5), * P5, K15, rep from * to last 22(12) sts, P5, K15(5), P1, K1.
Rows 11 to 14: Rep rows 9 and 10 twice.
Rows 15 to 22: Rep rows 1 and 2 four times.
Row 23: K2, P5(15), * K5, P15, rep from * to last 12(22) sts, K5, P5(15), K2.
Row 24: K1, P1, K5(15), * P5, K15, rep from * to last 12(22) sts, P5, K5(15), P1, K1.
Rows 25 to 28: Rep rows 23 and 24 twice.
These 28 rows form the pat.
Continue in pat until back measures approximately 10¼(11½)" from beg, ending with row 18(4).
Shape neck
Next row: Pat across 35(41) sts, turn and leave remaining sts on a spare needle.
Keeping pat correct, dec 1 st at neck edge on every row until 27(33) sts remain.
Now bind off.
Return to sts on spare needle.
With right side facing, slip first 29(37) sts onto a holder, rejoin yarn to next st and using smaller needles, work in seed st (see page 133) to end of row.
Continuing in seed st, dec 1 st at neck edge on every row until 27(33) sts remain.
Now bind off.

FRONT
Work as for back until 22 rows less than back to shoulders have been worked, ending with row 6(20).
Shape neck
Next row: Pat across 39(45) sts, turn and leave remaining sts on a spare needle.
Keeping pat correct, dec 1 st at neck edge on every row until 27(33) sts remain.
Work straight until front measures same as back to shoulders.
Change to smaller needles and work buttonhole border as follows:
Work 4 rows seed st.
Next row (buttonhole row): Seed st 7(9), * yo, sl 1, K1 psso, seed st 6(8), rep from * once more, yo, sl 1, K1, psso, seed st 2.
Work 3 rows seed st.
Bind off.
Return to sts on spare needle.
With right side facing, slip first 21(29) sts onto a holder, rejoin yarn and pat to end.
Keeping pat correct, dec 1 st at neck edge on every row until 27(33) sts remain.
Work straight until front measures same as back to right shoulder, ending with a wrong-side row.
Bind off.

This clever basket-weave effect is created by combining stockinette stitch, reverse stockinette stitch and seed stitch. The result is a warm little sweater with a lot of stretch in it!

SLEEVES

Using smaller needles cast on 46(54) sts.
Work 1½" rib as for back ending with rib row 1.
Inc row: Rib 4(2), * in in next st, rib 2(11), rep from * to last 5(3) sts, inc in next st, rib 4(2): 59 sts.
Change to larger needles.
Now working in pat as for first size of back, inc and work into pat 1 st within the 2 st border at each end of 5th and every following 4th row until there are 79(89) sts.
Work straight until sleeve measures approximately 8¼(9)" from beg, ending with row 28(8).
Bind off.

NECKBAND

With right side facing and using smaller needles, pick up and K26 sts down left side of front neck, K across 21(29) sts on front neck holder, pick up and K18 sts up right side of front neck and 8 sts down right side of back neck, K across 29(37) sts on back neck holder, then pick up and K8 sts up left side of back neck: 110(126) sts. Now P 1 row.
Work 5 rows in rib as for back.
Buttonhole row: Rib to last 5 sts, P2 tog, yo, rib to end.
Work 5 more rows in rib.
Bind off.

TO FINISH

Block if necessary, but do not press.
Overlap buttonhole border on left shoulder and catch together at armhole edge. Sew in sleeves, then join side and sleeve seams. Sew on buttons.

EGG COSIES

Three Easter egg cosies.

MATERIALS

Small amounts of lightweight smooth yarn
For the Rabbit
Gray main, white contrasting
For the Mouse
Pink main, white contrasting
For the Chicken
White main, red contrasting
Also a short length of black for embroidery on the Rabbit and Mouse
A pair each of size 2, size 3 and size 4 knitting needles

INSTRUCTIONS

BASIC COSY

Using largest needles and 2 strands of main color yarn together, cast on 39 sts.
Rib row 1: K1, * P1, K1, rep from * to end.
Rib row 2: P1, * K1, P1, rep from * to end.
Rep these 2 rows twice more, inc 1 st at end of last row: 40 sts.
Beg with a K row, work 10 rows st st.
Shape Top
Row 1: * K5, K2 tog, rep from * to last 5 sts, K5: 35 sts.
Row 2 and every other row: P.
Row 3: * K4, K2 tog, rep from * to last 5 sts, K5: 30 sts.
Row 5: * K3, K2 tog, rep from * to end: 24 sts.
Row 7: K2, K2 tog, rep from * to end: 18 sts.
Row 8: P.
For Rabbit and Mouse: Break off yarn and thread through sts, draw up tightly, then fasten off securely and join back seam.
For Chicken: Divide the sts onto 2 needles with both points facing the same way, then slip 1 st from each needle onto a 3rd needle, pass the first of these 2 sts on the 3rd needle over the 2nd and off the needle, continue in this way to end of row: 9 sts. Break off yarn. Join back seam.

RABBIT'S EARS (make 2)

Using medium-size needles and 1 strand of main color yarn, cast on 12 sts.
Beg with a K row, work 20 rows st st.
Dec 1 st each end of next and every other row until 4 sts remain.
Change to smallest needles and contrasting color for ear linings.
Inc 1 st each end of next and every other row until there are 12 sts.
Work 20 rows straight. Now bind off.
Join seams at sides of ears, fold ear at base and sew in place on cosy.

These English table accessories are practical as well as amusing: they keep soft-boiled eggs warm until they reach the table.

TO FINISH RABBIT

Using contrasting color, make a pompom by winding yarn around two fingers about 40 times, secure tightly around center, then cut loops and fluff up. Sew pompom in place, then embroider rabbit's features as shown in picture.

MOUSE'S EARS (make 2)

Using medium-size needles and 1 strand of main color yarn, cast on 6 sts.
Working in st st, inc 1 st each end of first and every other row until there are 12 sts.
Work 7 rows straight.
Dec 1 st each end of next 3 rows, work 1 row straight.
Change to smallest needles and contrasting color for ear linings.
Work 1 row.
Inc 1 st each end of next 3 rows: 12 sts.
Work 6 rows straight, then dec 1 st each end of next and every other row until 6 sts remain.
Work 1 row and bind off.
Join seams at sides of ears, then gathering ear slightly at base, sew in place on cosy

MOUSE'S TAIL

Using medium-size needles and 2 strands of main color, cast on 26 sts, then bind off. Sew in place.

TO FINISH MOUSE

Embroider features as shown in picture.

CHICKEN'S CREST

Using medium-size needles and 1 strand of contrasting color and working across 9 sts on needle, K into front and back of each st to last st, K1: 17 sts.
Next row: P.
Working in st st, inc 1 st each end of next row and every other row twice: 23 sts.
Next row: K1, ✷ yo, sl 1, K1, psso, rep from ✷ to end.
Dec 1 st each end of next and every other row until 17 sts remain. Bind off.
Fold crest along row of holes and sew down bound-off edge and join side seams.

CHICKEN'S BEAK

Using medium-size needles and 1 strand of contrasting color, cast on 10 sts.
Working in st st, dec 1 st each end of 3rd and every other row until 4 sts remain.
Next row: P2 tog twice.
Break off yarn and thread through sts. Fold beak in half and join seam, then sew in place on cosy.

TO FINISH CHICKEN

Embroider eyes as in picture.

CIRCUS TIME

Bring on the clowns ... and the marching elephants, and the seals, and the balloons! This chapter contains a host of colorful, and exciting designs to knit for babies, toddlers, and, of course, Teddy. All are inspired by the circus ring, including Pierrot pullovers, an abstract cardigan, and a giant snake. With these and more, the following pages are full of surprises.

BIG TOP

A smart bomber jacket-style cardigan in a brilliantly colored abstract design.

MEASUREMENTS
To fit 22(24,25)" chest
Actual measurements 25(27,28½)"
Length from shoulder 12½(14,15)"
Sleeve seam 10¼(11,12½)"

MATERIALS
4(4,6)oz (100[100,150]g) of a smooth medium-weight yarn, such as Pingouin 4 Pingouins, in A
4oz (100g) of same in each of contrasting colors B and C
2oz (50g) of same in each of contrasting colors D and E
A pair each of size 2 and size 4 knitting needles
6 buttons

GAUGE
24 sts and 28 rows to 4" measured over st st worked on larger needles

To save time, take time to check gauge.

INSTRUCTIONS

BACK
Using smaller needles and A, cast on 72(76,80)sts.

This spectacular circus cardigan has all the color and razzmatazz of the Big Top. The eye-catching combination of abstract shapes and bold colors is one that children will adore.

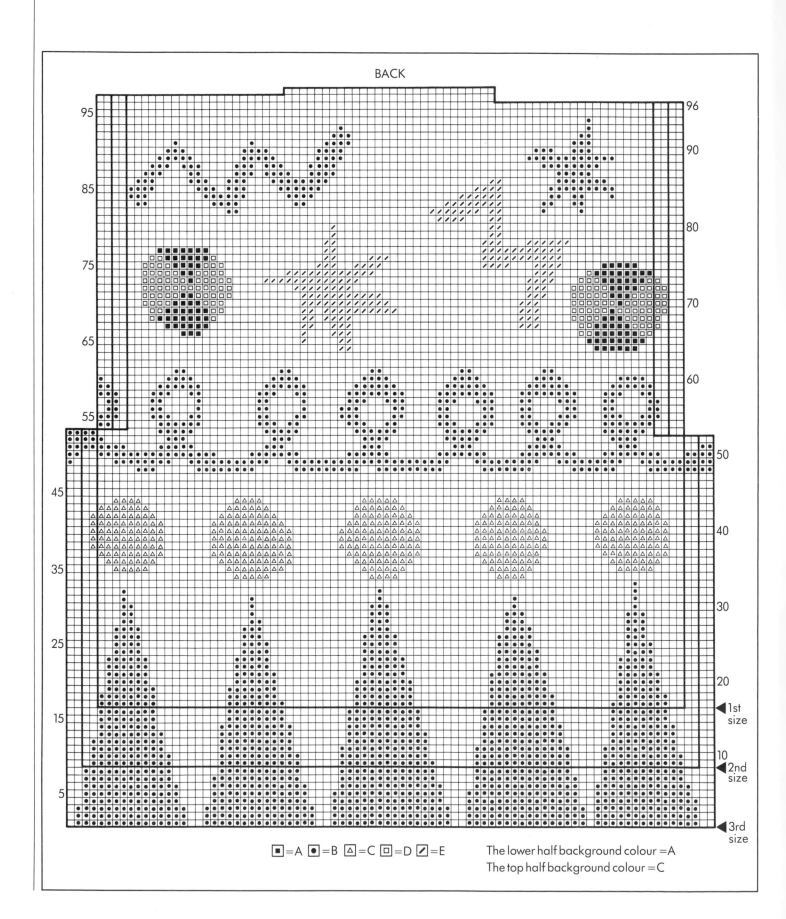

■=A ●=B △=C ▣=D ⁄=E   The lower half background colour =A
The top half background colour =C

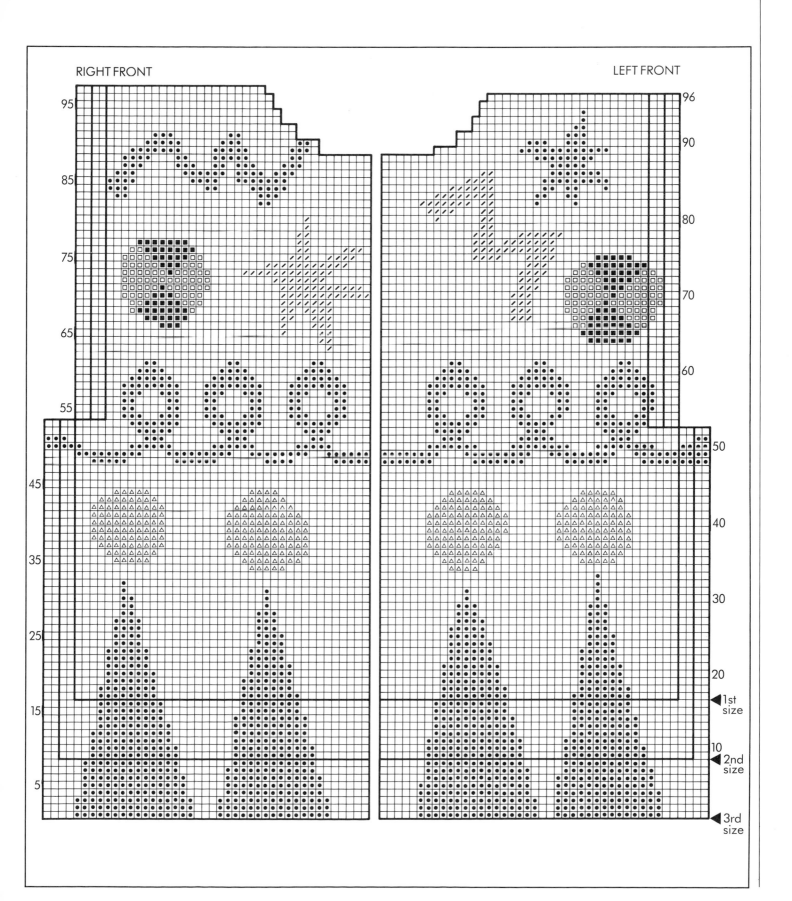

RIGHT FRONT

LEFT FRONT

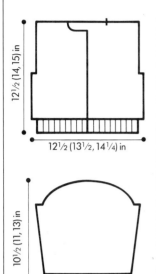

12½ (14, 15) in

12½ (13½, 14¼) in

10½ (11, 13) in

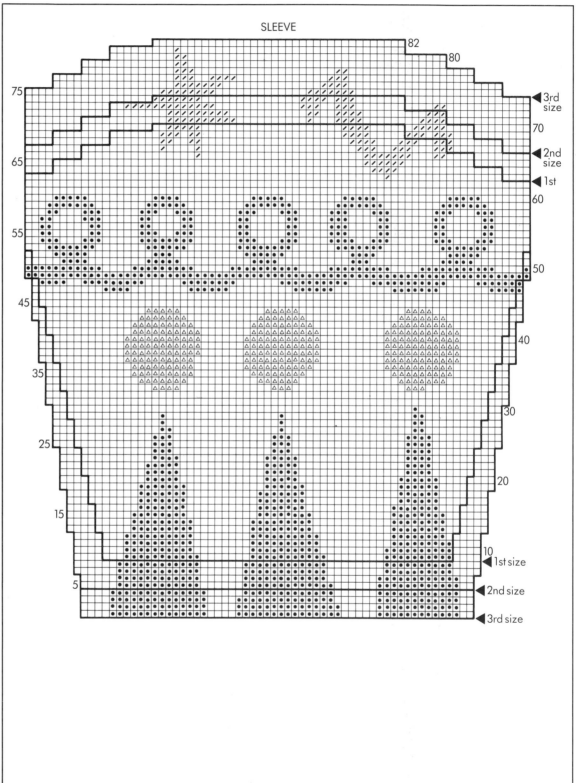

SLEEVE

The back of this stunning cardigan is as exciting as the front. Notice that the abstract shapes are not regular, so follow the charts carefully for an exact result.

Work 1½" in K1, P1 rib, ending with a right-side row.
Inc row: P11(10,10), ☆ inc in next st, P9(10,11), rep from ☆ to last 11(11,10)sts, inc in next st, P to end: 78(82,86)sts. Change to larger needles.
Reading odd-numbered (K) rows from right to left and even-numbered (P) rows from left to right, work in pat from chart for back, working armhole and shoulder shaping as indicated.

RIGHT FRONT
Using smaller needles and A, cast on 36(38,40)sts.
Work 1½" in K1, P1 rib, ending with a right-side row.
Inc row: P8, [inc in next st, P9] twice, inc in next st, P7(9,11): 39(41,43)sts.
Change to larger needles.
Work in pat from chart for right front, working armhole and neck shaping as indicated.

LEFT FRONT
Work as for right front, following chart for left front.

SLEEVES
Using smaller needles and A, cast on 42(48,48)sts.
Work 2½" in K1, P1 rib, ending with a right-side row.
Inc row: P6, ☆ inc in next st, P5(4,4), rep from ☆ to last 6(7,7)sts, inc in next st, P5(6,6): 48(56,56)sts.
Change to larger needles.
Work in pat from chart for sleeve, working increases as indicated.

BUTTONHOLE BORDER
With right side facing, using smaller needles and A, pick up and K74(84,94)sts up right front to beg of neck shaping.
Work 3 rows K1, P1 rib.
Buttonhole row (right side): Rib 4, ☆ yo, P2 tog, rib 10(12,14), rep from ☆ to last 8 sts, yo, P2 tog, rib to end.
Rib 3 more rows.
Bind off in rib.

BUTTON BORDER
Work as for buttonhole border, picking up sts down left front edge and omitting buttonholes.

NECKBAND
Join shoulder seams.
With right side facing, using smaller needles and A, pick up and K6 sts across buttonhole border, 19 sts up right side of front neck, 28 sts across back neck, 19 sts down left side of front neck, then 6 sts across button border: 78 sts.
Work 1¼" in K1, P1 rib.
Bind off in rib.

TO FINISH
Press or block as appropriate for yarn used. Sew in sleeves, then join side and sleeve seams. Sew on buttons.

MONTY PYTHON

A cuddly toy snake — all five feet of him!

MEASUREMENTS
Length approximately 60"
Circumference 8"

MATERIALS
4oz (100g) of a lightweight smooth yarn such as
Pingouin Pingofine in main color A
2oz (50g) of same in each of contrasting colors B
and C
Small amount for mouth in contrasting color D
A pair each of size 1 and size 2 knitting needles
Washable stuffing

GAUGE
32 sts and 40 rows to 4" measured over st st worked
on smaller needles

To save time, take time to check gauge.

INSTRUCTIONS

TAIL
Using smaller needles and A, cast on 6 sts.
Working in st st throughout, inc 1 st each end of 7th
and every following 6th row until there are 32 sts.
Work 5 rows straight.
Break off yarn, then onto same needle holding the
sts, cast on and make another piece in the same
way, but do not break off yarn.
Next row: K the first 31 of first set of sts, K tog the last
st with the first st of second set of 32 sts, K to end: 63
sts.
Work 7 rows straight.
★ Change to larger needles and work in pat from
chart as follows:
Row 1: K1A, ★ 2B, 4A, rep from ★ to last 2 sts, 2B.
Row 2: P3B, ★ 2A, 4B, rep from ★ to end.
Continue in pat from chart until row 16 has been
completed. Change to smaller needles.
Work 12 rows st st in A. ★
The last 28 rows from ★ to ★ form the pat; rep them
13 more times, then the first 16 rows again.
Change to smaller needles. Work 6 rows in A.
Divide for head shaping
Next row: K30, inc in next st, turn and leave
remaining sts on a spare needle: 32 sts. Work 1 row.
Shape head
★★ Inc 1 st each end of next and every other row until
there are 40 sts.
Work 5 rows straight.
Dec 1 st each end of next and every other row until
12 sts remain, ending with a P row. ★★
Bind off.

Return to remaining sts.
With right side facing, rejoin A to first st and K to end:
32 sts.
Work 1 row.
Now shape head as for first side from ★★ to ★★ .
Break off A and join on D.
Shape mouth lining
Continuing in st st, work 2 rows.
Inc 1 st each end of next and every other row until
there are 40 sts.
Work 25 rows straight, so ending with a P row.
Dec 1 st each end of next and every other row until
12 sts remain.
Bind off.

TONGUE
Using smaller needles and 2 strands of B together,
cast on 32 sts.
K 2 rows.
Next row: Bind off 8 sts, K to end. K 1 row.
Next row: Cast on 8 sts, K to end. K 1 row. Bind off.

TO FINISH
Duplicate stitch eyes as shown on chart, working
them 6 sts apart in line with the mouth. Join bound-
off edge of outer head to bound-off sts of lining.
Matching patterns, join tail and side seams leaving a
small opening for stuffing. Join lining for mouth to
sides of head, stuff lightly then catch lining in place
at back of throat. Sew in tongue. Stuff tail and body,
then neatly close opening.

 Monty is a cuddly knit-
ted snake that children
love to wind around their necks
(without the stuffing he could
double as a scarf). A lovable toy,
he can't bite but is sometimes
heard to hiss affectionately!

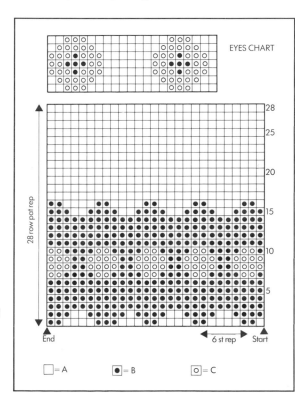

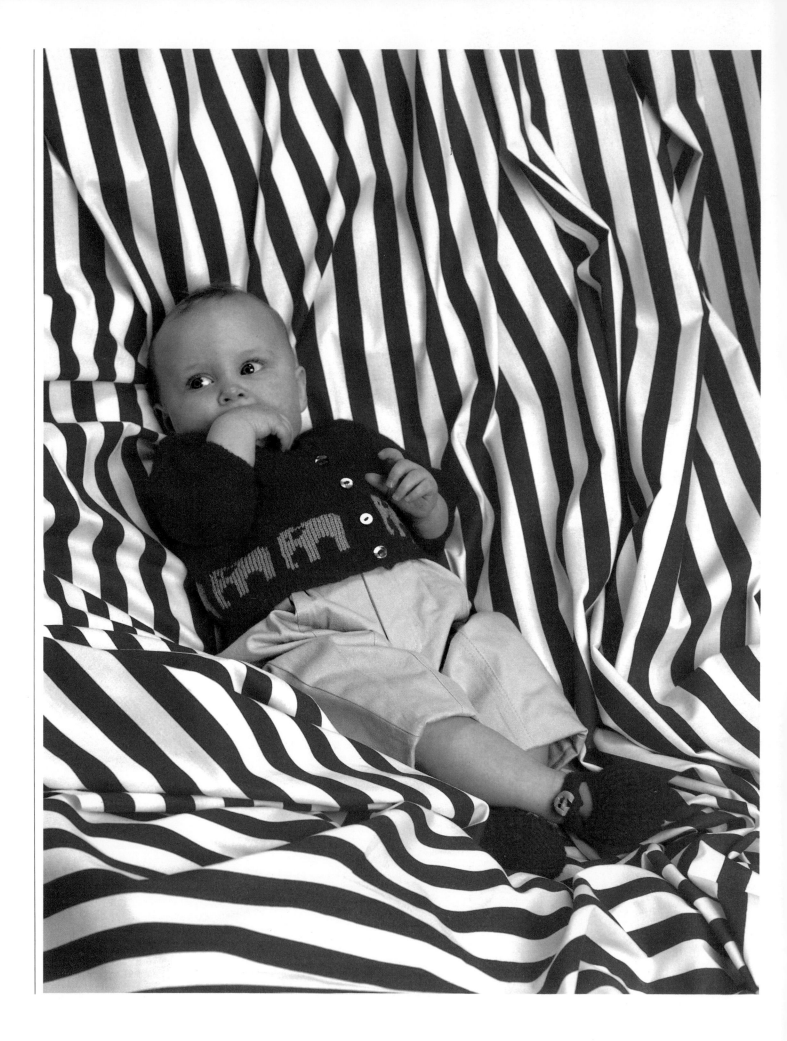

NELLIE THE ELEPHANT

Baby's cardigan with marching elephants around the bottom and matching bootees.

MEASUREMENTS

Cardigan
To fit 16–18" chest
Actual measurement 20"
Length from shoulder 10"
Sleeve seam 5¼"

Bootees
To fit 0–6 months

MATERIALS

Cardigan
4 oz (100 g) of a smooth lightweight yarn, such as Phildar Luxe, in main color A
2 oz (50 g) of same in contrasting color B
A pair each of size 0 and size 1 knitting needles
6 buttons

Bootees
2oz (50g) of same in color A
2 buttons, 3 stitch holders

GAUGE

32 sts and 36 rows to 4" measured over st st worked on medium-size needles

To save time, take time to check gauge.

INSTRUCTIONS FOR CARDIGAN

BACK AND FRONT

(worked in one piece to armholes)
Using smallest needles and A, cast on 177 sts.
Rib row 1: K2, * P1, K1, rep from * to last st, K1.
Rib row 2: K1, * P1, K1, rep from * to end.
Rep these 2 rows twice more.
Next row (buttonhole row): K2, P1, yo, P2 tog, rib to end.
Beg with rib row 2, work 3 more rows in rib.
Next row: Rib 7 and slip these sts onto a safety-pin, change to medium-size needles and K to last 7 sts, turn and leave remaining sts on a safety-pin: 163 sts.
Beg with a P row, work 3 rows st st.
Change to largest needles.
Work elephant motifs from chart as follows:
Row 1: K3A, [3B, 5A, 3B, 3A, 2B, 4A] 8 times.
Row 2: P3A, [3B, 3A, 3B, 5A, 3B, 3A] 8 times.
Continue in pat from chart until row 16 has been completed. Change to medium-size needles.
Continue in st st until work measures 6" from beg, ending with a P row.

Divide for back and fronts

Next row: K40 and slip these sts onto a holder for right front, K the next 83 sts, turn and leave

remaining 40 sts on a holder for left front.
Working on sts for back, bind off 5 sts at beg of next 2 rows.
Work 1 row.
Next row: K2, K2 tog tbl, K to last 4 sts, K2 tog, K2.
Next row: P.
Rep the last 2 rows until 61 sts remain.
Work straight until back measures 10" from beg, ending with a P row.

Shape shoulders

Bind off 19 sts at beg of next 2 rows.
Break off yarn and leave remaining 23 sts on a holder. Return to sts on holder for right front.
With wrong side facing, join on A, bind off 5 sts, then P to end: 35 sts.
★ Dec 1 st at armhole edge as for back on next and every other row until 29 sts remain.
Work straight until front measures 8" from beg, ending at front edge.
Next row: Work across first 4 sts then slip these sts onto a safety-pin, work to end.
Work 1 row.
Dec 1 st at neck edge on next and every other row until 19 sts remain.
Work straight until front measures same as back to shoulders, ending with a P row.
Bind off. ★
Return to sts on holder for left front.
With right side facing, join on A, bind off 5 sts, then K to end: 35 sts. Work 1 row.
Now complete as for right front from ★ to ★.

SLEEVES

Using smallest needles and A, cast on 43 sts.
Work 10 rows rib as for back and fronts.
Change to largest needles.
Inc row: K1, * inc into next st, K1, rep from * to end: 64 sts.
Working in st st, inc 1 st each end of 11th and every following 10th row until there are 70 sts.
Work straight until sleeve measures 5¼" from beg, ending with a P row.

Shape top

Bind off 5 sts at beg of next 2 rows.
Working shaping as for back, dec 1 st each end of next and every other row until 48 sts remain, ending with a P row.
Bind off 6 sts at beg of next 4 rows: 24 sts.
Bind off.

BUTTON BORDER

With right side facing, slip the 7 sts on holder at lower edge of left front onto a smallest-size needle, join on A, inc into first st, [K1,P1] twice, K2: 8 sts.
Next row: [K1, P1] 4 times.
Continue in rib until border, when slightly stretched, fits up front to beg of neck shaping. Break off yarn and leave sts on holder. Sew on the border and

A delightful cardigan and bootee set featuring marching elephants; the baby's cardigan is hardly jumbo-sized, but these boots were made for walking!

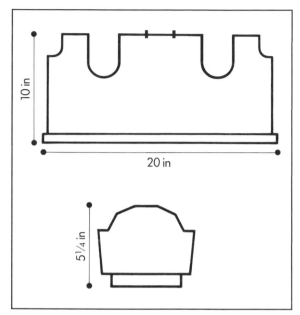

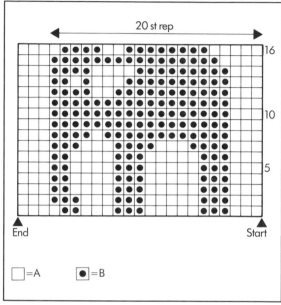

=A   =B

mark the position for 5 buttons, the first one to match first buttonhole, the top one 1¼" from top of border and the others spaced evenly in between.

BUTTONHOLE BORDER

With wrong side facing, slip the 7 sts on holder at lower edge of right front onto a smallest-size needle, join on A, inc into first st, [P1, K1] 3 times.
Next row: K2, [P1, K1] 3 times.
Complete as for button border, working buttonholes opposite markers as follows:
Buttonhole row (right side): K2, P1 yo, P2 tog, K1, P1, K1.

NECKBAND

Sew on buttonhole border and join shoulder seams. With right side facing, using smallest needles and A, rib across 7 sts of buttonhole border, K the last st of buttonhole border together with first of 4 sts on safety-pin at right front neck, K the next 3 sts, pick up and K16 sts up right front neck, K across 23 sts from back neck holder, pick up and K16 sts down left front neck, K 3 sts from safety-pin at left front and K the last st on safety-pin together with first st from button border, then rib 7: 77 sts.
Next row (wrong side): K1, * P1, K1, rep from * to end.
Buttonhole row: K2, P1, yo, P2 tog, rib to end.
Work 11 more rows rib, making a 2nd buttonhole on 8th row. Bind off in rib.

TO FINISH

Press or block as appropriate for yarn used. Fold neckband in half to wrong side and slipstitch in place.
Join sleeve seams, then sew in sleeves.

INSTRUCTIONS FOR BOOTEES

Using largest needles and 2 strands of yarn together throughout, cast on 31 sts.
K 1 row.
Shape sole
Row 1 (right side): Inc in first st, K14, inc in next st, K14, inc in last st.
Row 2 and every other row: K to end.
Row 3: Inc in first st, K15, inc in next st, K16, inc in last st.
Row 5: Inc in first st, K17, inc in next st, K17, inc in last st.
Row 7: Inc in first st, K18, inc in next st, K19, inc in last st.
Row 9: Inc in first st, K20, inc in next st, K20, inc in last st.
Row 11: Inc in first st, K21, inc in next st, K22, inc in last st: 49 sts.
Row 12: K to end.
Work in pat as follows:
Row 1 (right side): K1, * yfwd sl 1 pw, yo, K1, rep from * to end.
Row 2: K1, K2 tog, * yfwd, sl 1 pw, yo, K2 tog, rep from * to last st, K1.
Row 3: K1, * yfwd, sl 1 pw, yo, K2 tog, rep from * to last 2 sts, yfwd, sl 1 pw, yo, K1.
Rep rows 2 and 3 five more times, then work row 2 again.
Next row (right side): K2, * K2 tog, K1, rep from * to last 4 sts, K2 tog, K2.
Next row: K20, [K2 tog] twice, K1, [K2 tog] twice, K20.
Next row: K18, [K2 tog] twice, K1, [K2 tog] twice, K18.
Next row: K16, [K2 tog] twice, K1, [K2 tog] twice, K16.

*"Nellie the elephant packed
her trunk,
And trundled off to the circus,
Off she went with a trumpetty
trump,
Trump, trump, trump.*

*Night by night, she danced to
the circus band,
When Nellie was leading the
big parade
She looked so proud and
grand.*

*No more tricks for Nellie to
perform,
They taught her how to take a
bow
And she took the crowd by
storm.*

*Nellie the elephant packed her
trunk,
And trundled back to the
jungle,
Off she went with a trumpetty
trump,
Trump, trump, trump."*

Next row: K14, [K2 tog] twice, K1, [K2 tog] twice, K14: 33 sts.
Next row: K10, bind off 13 sts, K to end.
Work on first set of 10 sts for button strap.
Next row: K to end.
Next row: Cast on 8 sts, K to end: 18 sts. K 3 rows.
(For 2nd bootee, work buttonhole on first of these rows.)
Bind off.
With right side facing, join yarn to remaining 10 sts, cast on 8 sts, then K to end: 18 sts.

K 1 row.
Next row (buttonhole row): K3, yo, skpo, K to end.
(For 2nd bootee, K this row.)
K 2 rows.
Bind off.
Make 2nd bootee in same way, reversing buttonhole on strap as indicated.

TO FINISH
Join sole and center back seam.
Sew on buttons.

HARLEQUIN

A colorful long-sleeved raglan pullover with a perky stand-up collar.

MEASUREMENTS
To fit 18(20,22)" chest
Actual measurements 22(24,26)"
Length from shoulder 10¾(11¾,13)"
Sleeve seam 7(8,9)"

MATERIALS
2oz (50g) of a smooth lightweight yarn, such as Pingouin Pingofine, in each of colors A, B, C and D
A pair each of size 1 and size 2 knitting needles. Set of four size 1 double-pointed needles.
Stitch holder.

GAUGE
32 sts and 40 rows to 4" measured over st st worked on larger needles

To save time, take time to check gauge.

INSTRUCTIONS

BACK
★ Using smaller needles and B, cast on 91(99,107)sts.
Rib row 1: K2, ★ P1, K1, rep from ★ to last st, K1.
Rib row 2: K1, ★ P1, K1, rep from ★ to end.
Rep these 2 rows for 1½", ending with rib row 2 and increasing 1 st at end of last row: 92(100,108)sts.
Change to larger needles. Break off B and join on D.
Beg with a K row, work in st st until back measures 6(6½,7½)" from beg, ending with a P row.
Shape raglans
Bind off 4 sts at beg of next 2 rows.
Work 2 rows straight. ★
Next row: K2, K2 tog, K to last 4 sts, skpo, K2.
Next row: P.
Rep these 2 rows until 36(40,44) sts remain, ending with a P row.
Break off yarn and leave sts on a holder.

FRONT
Using A instead of B and C instead of D, work as for back from ★ to ★.
Next row: K2, K2 tog, K to last 4 sts, skpo, K2.
Next row: P.
Rep these 2 rows until 54(58,62) sts remain, ending with a P row.
Shape neck
Next row: K2, K2 tog, K16, turn and leave remaining sts on a spare needle.
Continuing to dec at raglan edge as before, dec 1 st at neck edge on next 8 rows.
Keeping neck edge straight, dec at raglan edge as

before until 3 sts remain. Bind off.
Return to remaining sts.
With right side facing, slip the first 14(18,22)sts onto a holder, join on C and complete second side of neck to match first, reversing all shaping.

SLEEVES
Using smaller needles and D for right sleeve or C for left sleeve, cast on 53(53,61)sts.
Work 1½" rib as for back, increasing 1 st at end of last row: 54(54,62) sts.
Change to larger needles.
Break off yarn and join on A for right sleeve or B for left sleeve.
Beg with a K row, work in st st, increasing 1 st each end of 5th and every following 4th row to 62(62,68)sts, then every following 6th row until there are 74(74,82)sts.
Work straight until sleeve measures 7(8,9)" from beg, ending with a P row.
Shape raglan
Bind off 4 sts at beg of next 2 rows.
Next row: K2, K2 tog, K to last 4 sts, skpo, K2.
Next row: P.
Rep these 2 rows until 14(14,18)sts remain, ending with a P row. Break off yarn and leave sts on a holder.

COLLAR
Join raglan seams.
With right side facing, slip the first 7(9,11)sts from holder at center front neck onto a safety-pin; using set of double-pointed needles and A, K across remaining 7(9,11)sts from holder, pick up and K18 sts up right side of neck, K across 14(14,18)sts from right sleeve holder, 36(40,44)sts from back neck holder and 14(14,18)sts from left sleeve holder, pick up and K19 sts down left side of neck, then K across 7(9,11)sts from safety-pin: 116(124,140)sts.
Round 1: K1, ★ P1, K1, rep from ★ to end (forming K2 at center front). Rep this round for ¾".
Now continue in rows as follows:
Row 1: K1, ★ P1, K1, rep from ★ to end, turn.
Row 2: K2, ★ P1, K1, rep from ★ to last st, K1, turn.
Continue working backward and forward in rows until collar measures 2" from beg, ending with a wrong-side row. Bind off knitwise.

TO FINISH
Press or block as appropriate for yarn used. Join side and sleeve seams.

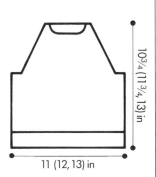

Perfect for wearing in the ring, these colorful Harlequin pullovers also look great on off-duty clowns with jeans, tracksuit bottoms, or skirts!

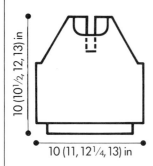

10 (10½, 12, 13) in

10 (11, 12¼, 13) in

10¼ (11¾, 14, 14½) in

PIERROT

A slightly fluffy raglan-sleeved pullover with an all-in-one ruff at the neck, ruffles at the cuffs, and dots or pompoms down the front.

MEASUREMENTS

To fit 16(18,20,22)" chest
Actual measurements 20(22,24,26)"
Length from shoulder 9¾(10½,12,13)"
Sleeve seam 6(7,8½,9)"

MATERIALS

2(4,6,6)oz (50[100,150,150]g) of a lightweight mohair-blend yarn, such as Phildar Anouchka, in main color A
2oz(50g) of same in contrasting color B
A pair each of size 1 and size 2 knitting needles
3 buttons, 3 stitch holders

GAUGE

28 sts and 36 rows to 4" measured over st st worked on larger needles

To save time, take time to check gauge.

INSTRUCTIONS

BACK

Using smaller needles and B, cast on 67(75,81,87) sts.
Row 1: K2, * P1, K1, rep from * to last st, K1.
Break off B and join on A.
Row 2: K1, P to last st, K1.
Row 3: K2, * P1, K1, rep from * to last st, K1.
Row 4: K1, * P1, K1, rep from * to end.
Rep rows 3 and 4 until work measures 1(1½,1½)" from beg, ending with row 3.
Inc row: Rib 14(16, 10, 8), [inc in next st, rib 11(13,11,13)sts] 3(3,5,5) times, inc in next st, rib to end: 71(79,87,93) sts. Change to larger needles.
Beg with a K row, work in st st until back measures 6¼(6¾,8,9)" from beg, ending with a P row.
Shape raglans
Bind off 2(3,3,4) sts at beg of next 2 rows.
Next row: K2, K2 tog, K to last 4 sts, skpo, K2.
Next row: P.
Rep last 2 rows until 57(59,61,65) sts remain, ending with a P row.
Divide for back opening
Next row: K2, K2 tog, K22(23,24,26), turn and leave remaining sts on a spare needle.
Keeping neck edge straight, continue dec at raglan edge as before until 11(12,13,15) sts remain.
Break off yarn and leave sts on a holder.
Return to remaining sts.
With right side facing, join on yarn and bind off the

first 5 sts, K to last 4 sts, skpo K2.
Now complete second side of neck to match first, reversing all shaping.

FRONT

Work as for back until 41(43,45,49) sts remain when shaping raglans.
Shape neck
Next row: K2, K2 tog, K13, turn and leave remaining sts on a spare needle.
Decreasing at raglan edge as before, dec 1 st at neck edge on next 8 rows.
Keeping neck edge straight, continue dec at raglan edge until 2 sts remain. Bind off.
Return to remaining sts.
With right side facing, slip first 7(9,11,15) sts onto a holder, join on yarn and complete to match first side of neck, reversing all shaping.

SLEEVES

For 1st size only
Using smaller needles and B, cast on 39 sts and work rows 1 and 2 as for back.
For 2nd, 3rd and 4th sizes only
Using larger needles and B, cast on (82,86,94) sts.
K1 row. Break off B and join on A.
Beg with a K row, work 7 rows st st.
Next row: * P2 tog, rep from * to end: (41,43,47) sts.
Change to smaller needles.
All sizes
Rep rows 3 and 4 as for back 5(5,6,6) times.
Change to larger needles.
Working in st st, inc 1 st each end of 5th(first,first,5th) and every following 4th row until there are 55(61,67,71) sts.
Work straight until sleeve measures 6¾(7,8½,9)" from beg, ending with a P row.
Shape raglan
Bind off 2(3,3,4) sts at beg of next 2 rows.
Next row: K2, K2 tog, K to last 4 sts, skpo, K2.
Next row: P.
Rep these 2 rows until 11(11,11,13) sts remain, ending with a P row.
Break off yarn and leave sts on a holder.

RUFFLE

For 2nd, 3rd and 4th sizes only
Using larger needles and B, cast on (166,174,198) sts. K1 row.
Break off B and join on A.
Beg with a K row, work 12 rows st st.
Next row: * K2 tog, rep from * to end of row: (83,87,99) sts.
Break off yarn and leave sts on needle.

NECKBAND

Join raglan seams.
With right side facing and using smaller needles and

Black and white used to be thought too severe for babies and small children. But these original Pierrot pullovers look stunning on small children, even though they call for black accessories.

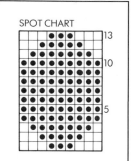

SPOT CHART

A, K across 11(12,13,15) sts from left back holder and 11(11,11,13) sts from left sleeve, pick up and K14 sts down left front neck, K across 7(9,11,15) sts from front neck holder, pick up and K14 sts up right front neck, then K across 11(11,11,13) sts from right sleeve holder and 11(12,13,15) sts from right back holder: 79(83,87,99) sts.

1st size only
Using B, P 1 row.
Next row: K2, ✷ P1, K1, rep from ✷ to last st, K1.
Break off B.
Continuing in A, P 1 row.

2nd, 3rd and 4th sizes only
Holding wrong side of ruffle to right side of neck, P together 1 st from neckband with 1 st from ruffle to end of row: (83,87,99) sts.

All sizes
Rib row 1: K2, ✷ P1, K1, rep from ✷ to last st, K1.
Rib row 2: K1, ✷ P1, K1, rep from ✷ to end.
Rep these 2 rows 3(6, 6, 6) more times.
Bind off in rib.

BUTTONHOLE BORDER
With right side facing and using smaller needles and A, pick up and K33(35,35,35) sts evenly down right back opening.
Row 1: K2, ✷ P1, K1, rep from ✷ to last st, K1.
Row 2: K1, ✷ P1, K1, rep from ✷ to end.
Row 3: As row 1.
Row 4: Keeping rib correct, rib 5, [yo, skpo, rib 8] twice, yo, skpo, rib 6(8,8,8).
Rows 5 and 6: As rows 1 and 2.
Row 7: As row 1.
Bind off purlwise.

BUTTON BORDER
Work as for buttonhole border, omitting buttonholes.

TO FINISH
Block the work.
Sew row ends of button and buttonhole borders in place over bound-off sts. Fold neckband in half to wrong side and slipstitch in place. Sew on buttons. Join side and sleeve seams.
For 1st size only
Placing motifs centrally as shown and using B, duplicate stitch dots to front of sweater.
For 2nd, 3rd and 4th sizes only
Using B, make 2 pompoms (see page 141) approximately 2" in size and sew them securely in place on front of sweater.

PIERROT DOLL

Pierrot himself — a knitted doll with separate costume.

MEASUREMENTS
Height approximately 13"

MATERIALS
Doll
2oz (50g) of a smooth lightweight yarn in main color A (White)
Small amounts of same in Black for feet, hat and eyes and Red for nose and mouth
Pierrot Costume
2oz (50g) of a lightweight mohair-blend yarn, such as Phildar Anouchka, in main color A (White)
Small amount of same in Black for edgings and pompoms
A pair each of size 2 and size 3 knitting needles
Size C crochet hook, 3 stitch holders
Washable stuffing, 1 button
Shirring elastic

GAUGE
Doll
26 sts and 36 rows to 4" measured over st st using larger needles and smooth yarn
Pierrot Costume
28 sts and 36 rows to 4" measured over st st using larger needles and mohair-blend yarn

To save time, take time to check gauge.

INSTRUCTIONS FOR DOLL

HEAD
Using larger needles and A, cast on 16 sts, P 1 row.
Shape head
Row 1 (right side): ✷ Inc in next st, K1, rep from ✷ to end: 24 sts.
Row 2: K1, P to last st, K1.
Rep these 2 rows twice more: 54 sts.
Work straight in st st until work measures 3" from beg, ending with a P row.
Shape neck
Row 1: [K1, K2 tog] 9 times, [K2 tog, K1] 9 times.
Row 2: K1, P to last st, K1.
Row 3: [K1, K2 tog] 6 times, [K2 tog, K1] 6 times.
Row 4: As row 2.
Row 5: [K1, K2 tog] 4 times, [K2 tog, K1] 4 times.
Row 6: K1, P to last st, K1: 16 sts.
Work 4 rows straight.
Shape body
Row 1: ✷ Inc in next st, K1, rep from ✷ to end: 24 sts.
Row 2: K1, P to last st, K1.
Rep these 2 rows twice more: 54 sts.
Work straight for 4½", ending with a P row.

Divide for legs

Next row: K27, turn and leave remaining sts on a spare needle.

★ Work straight until leg measures 3", ending with a P row.

Shape ankle

Next row: ★ K1, K2 tog, rep from ★ to end: 18 sts.
P1 row. Break off A, join on black.
K2 rows.
Beg with a K row, work 6 rows st st. ★

Shape foot

Next row: K8, turn and P4, turn and work 4 rows st st on these 4 sts, so ending with a P row.
Now K across the 4 sts, pick up and K3 sts down side of the 4 rows of st st, then K across remaining 10 sts: 17 sts.
Next row: P17, pick up and P3 sts down second side of 4 rows, then P remaining 4 sts: 24 sts.
Work 2 rows st st, then K 3 rows.
Bind off knitwise. Return to remaining sts.
With right side facing, rejoin A to first st and work as for first leg from ★ to ★.

Shape foot

Next row: K14, turn and P4, turn and work 4 rows st st on these 4 sts, so ending with a P row.
Now complete as for first leg, reversing all shaping.

ARMS

Using smaller needles and A, cast on 8 sts for shoulder.
Working in st st, inc 1 st each end of every row until there are 18 sts.
Work straight until arm measures 4½" from beg, ending with a P row.
Next row: ★ K2 tog, rep from ★ to end of row: 9 sts.
Break off yarn and thread through sts, draw up tightly and fasten off securely.

HAT

Using larger needles and black, cast on 56 sts.
K 5 rows. Beg with a K row, work 16 rows st st.

Shape crown

Row 1: ★ K2 tog, rep from ★ to end: 28 sts.
Row 2: P to end.
Rep these 2 rows once more: 14 sts.
Break off yarn and thread through sts, draw up tightly and fasten off securely.

TO FINISH

Using backstitch and black, embroider the outer line of eyes on face. Working from chart, duplicate stitch center of eyes, eyebrows, nose and mouth on face. Join feet and leg seams, then head, neck and back, leaving a small opening. Turn body right side out, stuff as firmly as desired, then close opening. Join arm seams, turn right side out, then stuff and sew in place. Join seam at back of hat, then slipstitch to head.

INSTRUCTIONS FOR PIERROT COSTUME

FRONT

★ Using smaller needles and black, cast on 25 sts for right leg.
K 1 row.
Break off black and join on A.
Beg with a K row, work in st st until leg measures 3" ending with a P row.
Break off yarn and leave sts on a spare needle.
Work left leg in same way, but do not break off yarn.
Next row: K25 sts of left leg, then K25 sts of right leg from spare needle: 50 sts.
Beg with a P row, work in st st until front measures 7" from beg, ending with a P row.

Shape raglans

Bind off 2 sts at beg of next 2 rows: 46 sts. ★
Next row: K2, K2 tog, K to last 4 sts, K2 tog tbl, K2.
Next row: P to end.
Rep these 2 rows until 10 sts remain, ending with a P row.
Break off yarn and leave sts on a holder.

BACK

Work as for front from ★ to ★.

Divide for back opening

Next row: K2, K2 tog, K19, turn and leave remaining sts on a spare needle.
Next row: P to end.
Next row: K2, K2 tog, K to end.
Rep these last 2 rows until 5 sts remain, ending with a P row.
Break off yarn and leave sts on a holder.

This is the smallest size of the Pierrot pullover, just to prove that small babies can wear black too. But, for a baby, add duplicate-stitched dots instead of pompons – they are harder to chew!

Practical cotton is a good choice for this mini tracksuit, which is perfect for crawling around in. Duplicate stitch the balloon motif all over if you prefer.

Return to remaining sts.
With right side facing, join on A, K to last 4 sts, K2 tog tbl, K2.
Next row: P to end.
Next row: K to last 4 sts, K2 tog tbl, K2.
Rep these last 2 rows until 5 sts remain, ending with a P row.
Break off yarn and leave sts on a holder.

SLEEVES

Using smaller needles and black, cast on 46 sts.
K 1 row.
Break off black and join on A.
Beg with a K row, work 6 rows st st.
Next row: ✻ K2 tog, rep from ✻ to end: 23 sts.
Now work in rib as follows:
Rib row 1: K1, ✻ P1, K1, rep from ✻ to end.
Rib row 2: K2, ✻ P1, K1, rep from ✻ to last st, K1.
Rep these 2 rows once more, the rib row 1 again.
Inc row: K into back and front of each st to end: 46 sts.
Next row: P to end.
Beg with a K row, work in st st until sleeve measures 3" from beg, ending with a P row.
Shape raglan
Bind off 2 sts at beg of next 2 rows: 42 sts.
Now dec as for front until 6 sts remain, ending with a P row.
Break off yarn and leave sts on a holder.

RUFFLE

Using smaller needles and black, cast on 64 sts.
K 1 row.
Break off black and join on A.
Beg with a K row, work 12 rows st st.
Next row: ✻ K2 tog, rep from ✻ to end: 32 sts.
Break off yarn and leave sts on needle.

NECKBAND

Join raglan seams.
With right side facing and using smaller needles and A, K across the 5 sts on holder at left back neck, 6 sts from left sleeve, 10 sts across front, 6 sts from right sleeve and 5 sts from right back neck: 32 sts.
Now holding wrong side of ruffle to right side of neck, P together 1 st from neckband with 1 st from ruffle to end of row: 32 sts.
Work 4 rows K1, P1 rib. Bind off knitwise.

TO FINISH

Block the work. Join leg, side and sleeve seams. Join inside leg seams. Using crochet hook and A, work 2 rows single crochet around neck opening, working a button loop at top of right back neck.
Sew on button. Using black, make 2 small pompoms approximately ¾" across and sew to front as shown. Thread wrists and ankles with shirring elastic and gather slightly.

BALLOONS

Dotted tracksuits for baby and bear!

MEASUREMENTS
Child's tracksuit
To fit 20" chest
Actual measurements 22"
Length from shoulder 12½"
Sleeve seam 8"
Outside leg (waist to ankle) 21¼"
Teddy's tracksuit
To fit height 19"

MATERIALS
Child's tracksuit
23oz (650g) of a heavyweight cotton yarn, such as Rowan D.K. Cotton in main color A
Teddy's tracksuit
4oz (100g) of a smooth wool yarn, such as Rowan lightweight D.K., in main color A
2oz (50g) of same in contrasting color B
For both suits
Small amounts of 4 contrasting colors for dots
A pair each of size 5 and size 7 knitting needles for child's and a pair of size 3 knitting needles for teddy's tracksuit
3 buttons for each tracksuit
Waist length of elastic for each tracksuit
3 stitch holders

GAUGE
20 sts and 28 rows to 4" measured over st st worked on largest needles with cotton
22 sts and 28 rows to 4" measured over st st worked on largest needles with lightweight wool

To save time, take time to check gauge.

INSTRUCTIONS FOR CHILD'S TRACKSUIT

BACK
Using medium-size needles cast on 50 sts.
Rib row: ✻ K1 tbl, P1, rep from ✻ to end.
Rep this row 10 more times to form twisted rib.
Inc row: Rib 8, ✻ M1, rib 7, rep from ✻ to end: 56 sts.
Change to largest needles.
Beg with a K row, work in st st until back measures 12½" from beg, ending with a P row.
Shape shoulders
Bind off 18 sts at beg of next 2 rows.
Break off yarn and leave remaining 20 sts on a holder.

FRONT
Work as for back until 12 rows less than back to shoulders have been worked.

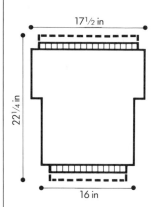

17½ in

22¼ in

16 in

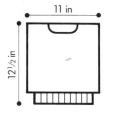

11 in

12½ in

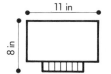

11 in

8 in

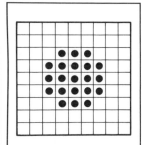

Shape neck

Next row: K22, K2 tog, turn and leave remaining sts on a holder.
Next row: P2 tog, P to end.
Next row: K to last 2 sts, K2 tog.
Rep the last 2 rows once more: 19 sts.
Next row: P to end.
Next row: K to last 2 sts, K2 tog: 18 sts.
Next row: P.
Beg with a K row, work 4 rows st st.
Bind off.
Return to remaining sts.
With right side facing, slip first 8 sts onto a holder, join on yarn, K2 tog, K to end: 23 sts.
Now complete to match first side of neck, reversing all shaping.

SLEEVES

Using medium-size needles cast on 30 sts.
Work 11 rows in twisted rib as for back.
Inc row: K2, [M1, K1] 26 times, K2: 56 sts.
Change to largest needles.
Beg with a K row, work in st st until sleeve measures 8" from beg, ending with a P row. Bind off.

NECKBAND

Join right shoulder seam.
With right side facing and using medium-size needles, pick up and K12 sts down left side of front neck, K across 8 sts from front neck holder, pick up and K12 sts up right side of front neck, then K across 20 sts from back neck holder: 52 sts.
Work 12 rows in twisted rib as for back.
Bind off in rib.
Fold neckband in half to wrong side and slipstitch in place.

BUTTON BORDER

With right side facing and using medium-size needles, pick up and K22 sts across left shoulder and neckband edge.
Work 5 rows in twisted rib. Bind off in rib.

BUTTONHOLE BORDER

Work as for button border, placing 3 buttonholes on the 3rd row as follows:
Buttonhole row (wrong side): Rib 1, [K2 tog, yo, rib 6] twice, K2 tog, yo, rib 3.

TO FINISH

Press the work lightly.
Overlap buttonhole border over button border and catch together at shoulders. Fold sleeves in half, then placing center of top of sleeves at shoulder seams, sew in place.
Working from chart, duplicate stitch dot motifs as desired. Join side and sleeve seams. Sew on buttons.

PANTS

Right leg: Using medium-size needles cast on 40 sts.
Work 2½" in twisted rib, ending with a right-side row.
Inc row: K into back and front of each st to end: 80 sts.
Change to largest needles.
Beg with a K row, work in st st until leg measures 12¾" from beg, ending with a P row.
Shape crotch
Cast on 4 sts at beg of next 2 rows: 88 sts.
Continue in st st until work measures 22½" from beg, ending with a K row.
Next row (dec row): Sl 1, * P2 tog, P1, rep from * to end: 59 sts.
Change to medium-size needles.
Rib row 1: K1 tbl, * P1, K1 tbl, rep from * to end.
Rib row 2: P1, * K1 tbl, P1, rep from * to end.
Rep these 2 rows for 2", ending with rib row 2.
Bind off in rib.
Left leg: Work as for right leg.

TO FINISH

Working from chart, duplicate stitch dot motifs as desired. Join front, back and inner leg seams. Fold ribbing at lower edge of legs to wrong side and slipstitch in place. Fold hem at top of pants in half to wrong side and slipstitch in place, leaving a small opening for elastic. Thread elastic into waistband, secure ends, then close opening.

INSTRUCTIONS FOR TEDDY'S TRACKSUIT

BACK

Using smallest needles and B, cast on 46 sts.
Rib row: * K1 tbl, P1, rep from * to end.
Rep this row 6 more times to form twisted rib.
Inc row: Rib 6, * M1, rib 4, rep from * to end: 56 sts.
Break off B and join on A.
Change to largest needles.
Beg with a K row, work in st st until back measures 7" from beg, ending with a P row.
Shape shoulders
Bind off 18 sts at beg of next 2 rows.
Break off yarn and leave remaining 20 sts on a holder.

FRONT

Work as for back until 12 rows less than back to shoulders have been worked.
Shape neck
Next row: K22, K2 tog, turn and leave remaining sts on a holder.
Next row: P2 tog, P to end.
Next row: K to last 2 sts, K2 tog.
Rep the last 2 rows once more: 19 sts.
Next row: P to end.
Next row: K to last 2 sts, K2 tog: 18 sts.
Next row: P.

Beg with a K row, work 4 rows st st.
Bind off. Return to remaining sts.
With right side facing, slip first 8 sts onto a holder, join on yarn, K2 tog, K to end: 23 sts.
Now complete to match first side of neck, reversing all shaping.

SLEEVES

Using smallest needles and B, cast on 28 sts.
Work 3 rows in twisted rib as for back.
Inc row: K3, [M1, K1] 22 times, K3: 50 sts.
Break off B and join on A.
Change to largest needles.
Beg with a K row, work in st st until sleeve measures 3" from beg, ending with a P row.
Break off A and join on B. K 3 rows. Bind off.

NECKBAND

Join right shoulder seam.
With right side facing and using smallest needles and B, pick up and K14 sts down left side of front neck, K across 8 sts from front neck holder, pick up and K14 sts up right side of front neck, then K across 20 sts from back neck holder: 56 sts.
K 1 row, then work 10 rows in twisted rib as for back.
Bind off in rib.
Fold neckband in half to wrong side and slipstitch in place.

BUTTON BORDER

With right side facing and using smallest needles and B, pick up and K22 sts across left shoulder and neckband edge.
K 1 row, then work 45 rows in twisted rib.
Bind off in rib.

BUTTONHOLE BORDER

Work as for button border, placing 3 buttonholes on the 3rd row as follows:
Buttonhole row (wrong side): Rib 1, [K2 tog, yo, rib 6] twice, K2 tog, yo, rib 3.

TO FINISH

Lap buttonhole border over button border and catch together at shoulders. Fold sleeves in half, then placing center of top of sleeves at shoulder seams, sew in place. Working from chart, duplicate stitch dot motifs as desired. Join side and sleeve seams. Sew on buttons.

PANTS

Right leg: Using smallest needles and B, cast on 48 sts.
Work 1½" in twisted rib, ending with a wrong-side row. Break off B and join on A.
Change to largest needles.
Beg with a K row, work in st st until leg measures 6¼" from beg, ending with a P row.

Shape crotch

Cast on 5 sts at beg of next 2 rows: 58 sts.
Continue in st st until work measures 10" from beg, ending with a P row.
Break off A and join on B.
Change to smallest needles.
Work 1½" in twisted rib. Bind off in rib.
Left leg: Work as for right leg.

TO FINISH

Press or block, as appropriate for yarn used. Working from chart, duplicate stitch dot motifs as desired. Join front, back and inner leg seams. Fold ribbing at lower edge of legs to wrong side and slipstitch in place. Fold hem at top of pants in half to wrong side and slipstitch in place, leaving a small opening for elastic. Thread elastic into waistband, secure ends, then close opening.

Teddy's tracksuit has been designed in a lightweight double knitting woolen yarn, but you can substitute oddments of cotton from the child's tracksuit if you prefer. If you do change the yarn remember to check the gauge.

"POCKETS" TOP

This warm little sweater has a wide collar and lots of little pockets for circus animals and a clown.

MEASUREMENTS
To fit 22" chest
Actual measurements 24"
Length from shoulder 12½"
Sleeve seam 8½"

MATERIALS
9oz (250g) of a smooth heavyweight yarn, such as YarnWorks Merino Sport, in main color A
2oz (50g) of same in contrasting colors B, C and D
Small amounts of same in Purple, Orange, Pink, Yellow, Red and Blue for toys
Washable stuffing for toys
A pair each of size 5, size 7 and size 9 knitting needles
2 buttons
Medium sized crochet hook, 3 stitch holders

GAUGE
17 sts and 24 rows to 4" measured over st st worked on largest needles

To save time, take time to check gauge.

INSTRUCTIONS FOR SWEATER

POCKET LININGS (make 4)
Using largest needles and A, cast on 12 sts.
Work 12 rows st st.
Break off yarn and leave sts on a holder.

BACK
★ Using medium-size needles and B, cast on 44 sts.
Rib row: ★ K1 tbl, P1, rep from ★ to end.
Change to A and rep rib row 10 more times. ★
Inc row: Rib 8, ★ inc in next st, rib 3, rep from ★ to last 8 sts, inc in next st, rib to end: 52 sts.
Change to largest needles.
Beg with a K row, work 66 rows st st.
Bind off 16 sts at beg of next 2 rows. Break off yarn and leave remaining 20 sts on a holder.

FRONT
Work as for back from ★ to ★.
Inc row: Rib 6, ★ inc in next st, rib 3, rep from ★ to last 6 sts, inc in next st, rib to end: 53 sts.
Change to largest needles.
Beg with a K row, work 4 rows st st.
Using separate small balls of yarn for each area of color and twisting yarns together on wrong side of work when changing color to avoid making a hole, work colored pocket as follows:

Next row: K33A, 12C, 8A.
Next row: P8A, 12C, 33A.
Rep these 2 rows 5 more times. Break off C.
Next row: Using A only, K33, slip the next 12 sts in C onto a holder, then with right side facing K across the 12 sts of one pocket lining, K to end: 53 sts.
Beg with a P row, work 14 rows st st.
Next row: P35A, 12B, 6A.
Next row: K6A, 12B, 35A.
Rep these 2 rows 5 more times. Break off B.
Next row: Using A only, P35, slip the next 12 sts in B onto a holder, then with wrong side facing P across the 12 sts of second pocket lining, P to end: 53 sts.
Work 2 rows st st, so ending with a P row.
Divide for neck opening
Next row: K24 then slip these sts onto a holder, bind off the next 5 sts, then K to end: 24 sts.
Beg with a P row, work 9 rows st st.
Shape neck
Row 1: Bind off 3 sts, work to end.
Row 2: Work to end.
Row 3: Work 2 tog, work to end.
Row 4: Work to last 2 sts, work 2 tog.
Rows 5 and 6: As rows 3 and 4.
Row 7: As row 3.
Row 8: Work to end: 16 sts.
Work 2 rows straight, then bind off.
Return to remaining sts.
With wrong side facing, join A to first st and P to end.
Beg with a K row, work 9 rows st st.
Now complete 2nd side of neck to match first, reversing all shaping.

RIGHT SLEEVE
Using medium-size needles and B, cast on 28 sts.
Changing to A on the 2nd row, work 9 rows rib as for back.
Inc row: Rib 4, ★ inc in next st, rep from ★ to last 4 sts, rib to end: 48 sts.
Change to largest needles.
Beg with a K row, work 10 rows st st.
Place pocket as follows:
Next row: K18A, 12B, 18A.
Next row: P18A, 12B, 18A.
Rep these 2 rows 5 more times.
Break off B.
Next row: Working in A only, K18, slip the next 12 sts in B onto a holder, then K the 12 sts of 3rd pocket lining, K to end: 48 sts.
Work another 22 rows st st.
Break off A, join on D and K 1 row.
Bind off knitwise.

LEFT SLEEVE
Work as for right sleeve until 10 rows st st in A have been completed.
Work another 10 rows in A.
Place pocket as follows (next page):

More clowning around in the circus ring with these clever and unusual sweaters with their removable knitted toys. The detachable bow ties fasten onto one of the buttons with a loop of hat elastic.

Next row: K18A, 12C, 18A.
Complete pocket as for right sleeve, then work another 12 rows st st in A.
Break off A, join on D and K 1 row.
Bind off knitwise.

COLLAR

Using medium-size needles and A, cast on 66 sts.
Work in rib as for back for 2".
Change to largest needles and continue in rib until work measures 3".
Break off A, join on B and rib 1 row.
Bind off in rib.

NECKBAND

Join shoulder seams.
With right side facing and using medium-size needles and A, pick up and K14 sts up right side of front neck, K20 sts from back neck holder, then pick up and K14 sts down left side of front neck: 48 sts.

Work 3 rows in rib as for back.
Bind off in rib.

BUTTON BORDER

Using medium-size needles and D, cast on 5 sts.
Work 12 rows in rib as for back.
Bind off in rib.
Sew border to left side of neck opening.

BUTTONHOLE BORDER

With right side facing and using medium-size needles and D, pick up and K5 sts along bound-off sts at neck opening.
Rib 2 rows.
Buttonhole row: Rib 2, yo, K2 tog, K1.
Rib 5 rows.
Work a 2nd buttonhole row, then rib 2 more rows.
Bind off in rib.
Sew border in place, then slipstitch cast-on sts of button border to lower edge of buttonhole border.

These tiny knitted toys are just the right size to fit snuggly into the pockets. Knit them in grey or in bright contrasting colors.

POCKET TOPS

Lower pocket on front: With right side facing and using largest needles and D, K across sts from holder.
K 2 rows.
Bind off.
Work other pocket tops in the same way using C for the top pocket on front and right sleeve and B for left sleeve.

TO FINISH

Fold sleeves in half lengthwise, then placing folds at shoulder seams, sew in place. Join side and sleeve seams. Sew cast-on edge of collar to inside neck edge, Sew on buttons. Press or block as appropriate for yarn used.

INSTRUCTIONS FOR BOW TIE

Using largest needles and B, cast on 16 sts.
Work 16 rows st st.
Bind off.
Working from chart and using A, duplicate stitch dots on one half of bow tie.
Fold tie in half and slipstitch edges together.
Using a short length of A, wind yarn tightly around center of bow tie several times and fasten off securely at back.
Using a short length of elastic, make a loop on back of bow tie to attach to top button on neck of sweater.

INSTRUCTIONS FOR TOYS

All the toys are knitted in a heavyweight yarn using size 5 needles and are worked in stockinette stitch throughout.

CLOWN

Cast on 6 sts in purple and 6 sts in orange.
Keeping colors correct, work 12 rows.
Cast on 5 sts at beg of next 2 rows and work 8 rows.
Bind off 8 sts at beg of next 2 rows.
Change to pink.
Work 1 row.
Cast on 2 sts at beg of next 2 rows.
Work 6 rows.
Bind off 2 sts at beg of next 2 rows.
Work 1 row.
Bind off.
Work a second piece in the same way.

TO FINISH

Join 2 pieces together; stuff to desired firmness. In yellow cast on 6 sts and work 12 rows. Bind off. Fold in half and sew, then wind yarn tightly around center to form a bow tie and sew to neck of clown. Embroider French knots to form buttons, nose and eyes, then duplicate stitch mouth. Using a crochet hook, loop short lengths of orange to head to form hair.

ELEPHANT

Using gray cast on 12 sts.
Work 14 rows straight.
Cast on 2 sts at beg of next row.
Work 1 row.
Next row: Cast on 2, work to last 2 sts, work 2 tog.
Work 1 row.
Rep last 2 rows once more.
Next row: Cast on 6 sts; work to last 2 sts, work 2 tog.
Work 1 row.
Dec 1 st at end of next row.
Work 1 row.
Next row: Bind off 8 sts, work to last 2 sts, work 2 tog.
Work 1 row.
Dec 1 st each end of next row.
Work 1 row.
Next row: Bind off 2 sts, work to last 2 sts, work 2 tog.
Bind off.
Make a 2nd piece in the same way, reversing all shapings.
Ear: Using gray cast on 8 sts.
Work 4 rows.
Dec 1 st each end of next row; work 1 row; dec 1 st each end of next row; work 1 row.
Bind off.
Work another piece in the same way.

TO FINISH

Join 2 pieces together; stuff to desired firmness. Embroider French knot to form eye. Join ear pieces together and sew to side of head.

SEAL

Using gray cast on 12 sts.
Work 15 rows.
Dec 1 st at beg of next and every other row until 6 sts remain.
Work 1 row.
Bind off 2 sts at beg of next row.
Work 1 row. Bind off.
Make another piece in the same way, reversing all shaping.
Flipper: Using gray cast on 2 sts.
Work 2 rows.
Inc 1 st each end of next row; work 1 row; inc 1 st each end of next row: 6 sts.
Work 5 rows. Bind off.
Work another piece in the same way.

TO FINISH

Join 2 pieces together; stuff to desired firmness. Embroider French knot to form eye. Join flipper pieces together and sew to side of body. Make a small pompom in red (see page 141) and sew to nose for ball.

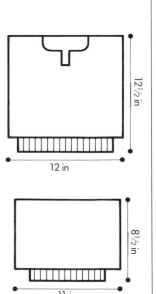

12½ in

12 in

8½ in

11 in

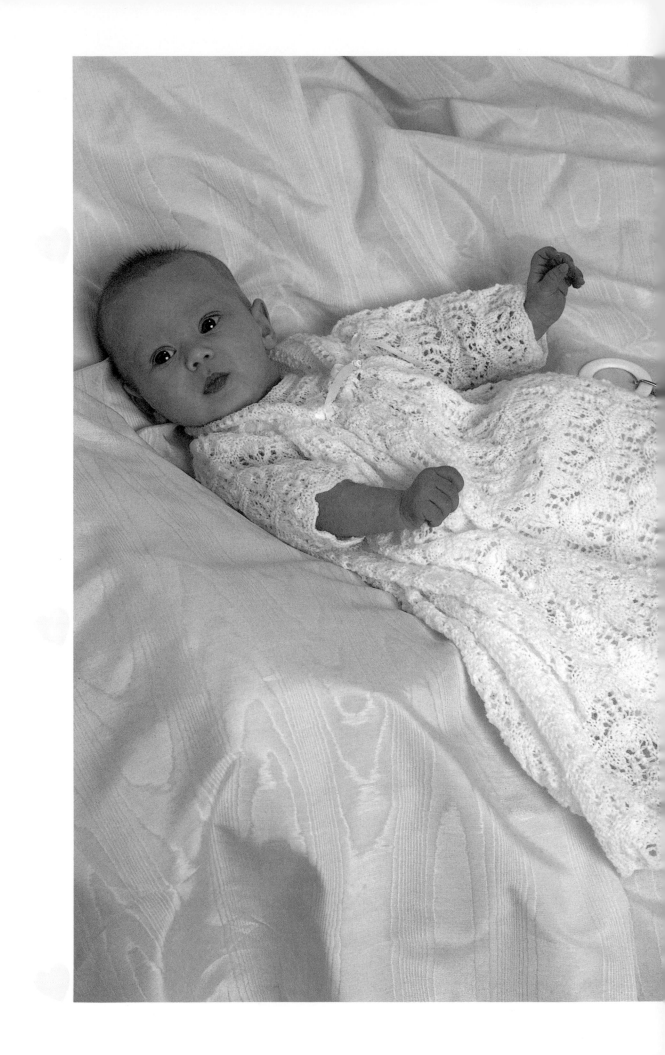

SPECIAL OCCASIONS

Whether it's a christening, a birthday or simply 'Sunday best', special occasions deserve clothes that are a little out of the ordinary. So the designs in this chapter are extra special. There is a delicate christening gown for that first special event, a smart Aran jacket and an adorable party bolero in gorgeous angora. Plus, of course, something for Teddy.

MONDAY'S CHILD

An exquisite design in delicate fingering yarn, for that special, special occasion.

MEASUREMENTS
To fit 18(19,20)" chest
Length from shoulder including yoke 22(23, 25)"
Sleeve seam 5½(6, 6¾)"

MATERIALS
5(5, 6) oz [120(120,160) g] of a fine fingering yarn, such as Sirdar Snuggly 2 ply
A pair each of size 2, size 3 and size 4 knitting needles
3 buttons; 1½ yd ribbon

GAUGE
1 pattern repeat (10 sts) measures 1½" worked on largest needles
10 rows to 2" measured over pattern worked on largest needles

To save time, take time to check gauge.

INSTRUCTIONS

BACK AND FRONT (alike)
Using largest needles cast on 153(163,173) sts.
Row 1: Sl 1, K to end.
Rows 2–5: As row 1.

A christening is a perfect excuse for some delicate lace-effect knitting. The patience such a design requires is well-invested considering the outstanding results.

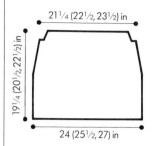

21¼ (22½, 23½) in

19¼ (20½, 22½) in

24 (25½, 27) in

7½ (7¾, 8½)

8½ (8½, 10¼)

Row 6: Sl 1, P1, ✶ yo, P3, P3 tog, P3, yo, P1, rep from ✶ to last st, K1.
Row 7: Sl 1, K2, ✶ yo, K2, sl 1, K2 tog, psso, K2, yo, K3, rep from ✶ to end.
Row 8: Sl 1, P3, ✶ yo, P1, P3 tog, P1, yo, P5, rep from ✶ to last 9 sts, yo, P1, P3 tog, P1, yo, P3, K1.
Row 9: Sl 1, K4, ✶ yo, sl 1, K2 tog, psso, yo, K7, rep from ✶ to last 8 sts, yo, sl 1, k2 tog, psso, yo, K5.
Row 10: Sl 1, P2, ✶ K2, P3, rep from ✶ to last 5 sts, K2, P2, K1.
Row 11: Sl 1, K1, ✶ yo, skpo, P1, yo, sl 1, K2 tog, psso, yo, P1, K2 tog, yo, K1, rep from ✶ to last st, K1.
Row 12: Sl 1, P3, ✶ K1, P3, K1, P5, rep from ✶ to last 9 sts, K1, P3, K1, P3, K1.
Row 13: Sl 1, K2, ✶ yo, skpo, yo, sl 1, K2 tog, psso, yo, K2 tog, yo, K3, rep from ✶ to end.
Row 14: Sl 1, P2, ✶ K1, P5, K1, P3, rep from ✶ to last 10 sts, K1, P5, K1, P2, K1.
Row 15: Sl 1, K2, ✶ P1, K1, yo, sl 1, K2 tog, psso, yo, K1, P1, K3, rep from ✶ to end.
Row 16: Sl 1, P2, ✶ K1, P5, K1, P3, rep from ✶ to last 10 sts, K1, P5, K1, P2, K1.
These 16 rows form the pat.
Continue in pat until work measures 10(10½, 12)" from beg, ending with a wrong-side row.
Change to medium-size needles.
Continue in pat until work measures 17½(18½, 20½)" from beg, ending with a wrong-side row.
Shape armholes
Bind off 8 sts at beg of next 2 rows.
Keeping pat correct, dec 1 st each end of next and every other row until 127(137,147) sts remain.
Break off yarn and leave these sts on a spare needle.

SLEEVES
Using medium-size needles cast on 63(63,73) sts.
Work in pat as for back and front until sleeve measures 5½(6, 6¾)" from beg, ending with a wrong-side row.
Shape top
Bind off 8 sts at beg of next 2 rows.
Keeping pat correct, dec 1 st each end of next and every other row until 37(37,47) sts remain.
Break off yarn and leave these sts on a spare needle.

YOKE
Block the work.
1st and 2nd sizes only
With right side facing slip the first 66(71) sts of back onto a holder, join yarn to next st and using medium-size needles cast on 5 sts, K across these 5 sts, then work across remaining 61(66) sts of back as follows: [K2 tog] 8(12) times, [K3 tog] 15(14) times; now work across 37 sts from top of first sleeve as follows: K1, [K2 tog, K2] 9 times; work across 127(137) sts of front as follows: [K3 tog] 13(12) times, [K2 tog]

23(31) times, [K3 tog] 14(13) times; work across 37 sts of second sleeve as follows: [K2, K2 tog] 9 times, K1; then work across 66(71) sts from holder on back as follows: [K3 tog] 15(14) times, [K2 tog] 8(12) times, K5: 162(174) sts.
3rd size only
With right side facing slip the first 76 sts of back onto a holder, join yarn to next st and using medium-size needles cast on 5 sts, K across these 5 sts, then work across remaining 71 sts of back as follows: [K2 tog] 16 times, [K3 tog] 13 times; now work across 47 sts from top of first sleeve as follows: [K2 tog] 5 times, [K1, K2 tog] 9 times, [K2 tog] 5 times; work across 147 sts of front as follows: [K3 tog] 11 times, [K2 tog] 39 times, [K3 tog] 12 times; work across 47 sts of second sleeve as follows: [K2 tog] 5 times, [K2 tog, K1] 9 times, [K2 tog] 5 times; then work across 76 sts from holder on back as follows: [K3 tog] 13 times, [K2 tog] 16 times, K5: 186 sts.
All sizes
Row 1: Sl 1, K to end.
Row 2: As row 1.
Row 3: Sl 1, K4, ✶ yo, P2 tog, rep from ✶ to last 5 sts, K5.
Rows 4–6: As row 1.
Row 7: Sl 1, K4, P to last 5 sts, K5.
Row 8: Sl 1, K4, [K1, K2 tog] 7(8,9) times, K31, [K2 tog, K1] 16(18,20) times, K31, [K2 tog, K1] 7(8,9) times, K5: 132(140,148) sts.
Row 9: Sl 1, K4, P to last 5 sts, K5.
Row 10: Sl 1, K to last 3 sts, yo, K2 tog, K1.
Rows 11 and 12: Rep row 1 twice.
Row 13: As row 3.
Rows 14–16: Rep row 1 three times.
Row 17: As row 7.
Row 18: Sl 1, K4, [K2 tog, K2] 12(13,14) times, [K2 tog, K3] 4 times, [K2 tog, K2] 13(14,15) times, K2 tog, K5: 102(108,114) sts.
Row 19: Sl 1, K4, P to last 5 sts, K5.
Row 20: Sl 1, K to last 3 sts, yo, K2 tog, K1.
Rows 21 and 22: Rep row 1 twice.
Row 23: As row 3.
Rows 24–26: Rep row 1 three times.
Row 27: As row 7.
Row 28: Sl 1, K4, [K2 tog, K3] 18(19,20) times, K2 tog, K5(6,7): 83(88,93) sts.
Row 29: Sl 1, K4, P to last 5 sts, K5.
Change to smallest needles.
Next row: Sl 1, K to last 3 sts, yo, K2 tog, K1.
Next row: Sl 1, K to end.
Rep the last row 3 more times.
Bind off.

TO FINISH
Join semi-raglan seams up to yoke. Join side and sleeve seams. Sew on buttons. Thread ribbon through first eyelet-hole row on yoke, keeping ends at the front. Tie into a bow at front.

SHELL SHAWL

This pretty shawl, which doubles as a blanket for a crib, uses three different colors. The shell effect gives a slightly raised and gathered texture.

MEASUREMENTS
Approximately 30" square

MATERIALS
6 oz[150 g] of a smooth lightweight yarn, such as Phildar Luxe in each of colors A, B and C
A pair of size 3 knitting needles; size B crochet hook

GAUGE
38 sts to 6" measured over shell pat

To save time, take time to check gauge.

The dimensions given are perfect for a shawl or crib blanket, but it could easily be made large enough for a toddler's bed by increasing the number of stitches worked.

A party pullover (opposite) with special effects: basically a simple round-neck sweater with a back button fastening, liberally covered in small bobbles.

SPECIAL ABBREVIATIONS

Shell 6, make a shell as follows: ✶ insert the crochet hook through front of the stitch 5 rows below (the row worked in color A) the 3rd stitch on left-hand needle and draw through a long loop, slip loop onto right-hand needle, K1, rep from ✶ 5 more times but always insert hook into the same stitch.

Shell 7, finish shell as follows: [P2 tog tbl] 3 times, P1, [P2 tog] 3 times.

SPECIAL NOTE

Always carry colors not in use up side of work, twisting yarns together at side of work on every row to avoid long loops.

INSTRUCTIONS

TO MAKE

Using A, cast on 192 sts.
K 1 row.
Rows 1–6: K with B.
Row 7: With A, K9, [shell 6, K8] 13 times, K1.
Row 8: With A, K2, [K7, shell 7] 13 times, K8.
Rows 9–14: K with C.
Row 15: With A, K2, [shell 6, K8] 13 times, shell 6, K2.
Row 16: With A, K2, [shell 7, K7] 13 times, shell 7, K1.
These 16 rows form the pat.
Continue in pat until shawl measures 30" from beg, ending with row 8.
Bind off purlwise.

TO FINISH

With right side facing, using the crochet hook and A, work 2 rows sc evenly along each side of shawl.
Block the work.

LOTS OF DOTS

So simple but so effective — round-neck pullovers sprinkled with dots.

MEASUREMENTS

Child's pullover
To fit 18(20,22)" chest
Actual measurements 21(23, 25)"
Length from shoulder 10¼(12, 13½)"
Sleeve seam 7(8¾, 10)" with cuff turned back
Teddy's pullover
To fit 16" chest

MATERIALS

Child's pullover
6 oz[150 g] of a baby yarn, such as Patons Fairytale 4 ply, in main color A
2 oz[50 g] of same in contrasting color B
Teddy's pullover
2 oz[50 g] of same in main color A
2 oz[50 g] of same in contrasting color B
For both pullovers
A pair each of size 2 and size 3 knitting needles
3 buttons.
2 stitch holders

GAUGE

28 sts and 36 rows to 4" measured over pattern worked on larger needles

To save time, take time to check gauge.

SPECIAL ABBREVIATION

MB, Make Bobble using B as follows: K into front, back, front, back and front again of next stitch, then slip the 2nd, 3rd, 4th and 5th stitches from right-hand needle over the first stitch and off the needle.

NOTE

To prevent long loops on back of work, always use a separate length of yarn for each bobble. Darn in all ends when finishing garment.

INSTRUCTIONS FOR CHILD'S PULLOVER

BACK

✶ Using smaller needles and A, cast on 63(69,77) sts.
Rib row 1: K1, ✶ P1, K1, rep from ✶ to end.
Rib row 2: P1, ✶ K1, P1, rep from ✶ to end.
Rep these 2 rows for 1½(1½, 2)", ending with rib row 1.
Inc row: Rib 4(2,6), ✶ M1, rib 5(6,6), rep from ✶ to last 4(1,5) sts, M1, rib to end: 75(81,89) sts.
Change to larger needles.
Joining on lengths of B as required, work in pat as follows:

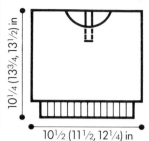

10¼ (13¾, 13½) in

10½ (11½, 12¼) in

8½ (10¼, 11¾) in

Row 1 (right side): K9(12,2) A, ✭ MB in B, K13 A, rep from ✭ to last 10(13,3) sts, MB in B, K9(12,2) A.
Row 2: P with A.
Row 3: K with A.
Row 4: P with A.
Rows 5–8: Rep rows 3 and 4 twice.
Row 9: K2(5,9) A, ✭ MB in B, K13 A, rep from ✭ to last 3(6,10) sts, MB in B, K2(5,9) A.
Row 10: P with A.
Rows 11–16: Rep rows 3 and 4 three times.
These 16 rows form the pat. ✭
Continue in pat until back measures 8(9½, 11)" from beg, ending with a wrong-side row.
Divide for back neck opening
Next row: Pat across 35(38,42) sts, turn and leave remaining sts on a spare needle.
Keeping pat correct, continue on these sts until back measures 10¼(12, 13½)" from beg, ending with a wrong-side row.
Next row: Bind off 23(26,29) sts, pat to end.
Break off yarn and leave remaining 12(12,13) sts on a holder. Return to remaining sts from spare needle.
With right side facing, slip first 5 sts onto a safety-pin, join yarn to remaining sts, pat to end.
Now complete to match first side of neck, reversing all shaping.

FRONT
Work as for back from ✭ to ✭.
Continue in pat until front measures 8¾(10½, 11½)" from beg, ending with a wrong-side row.
Shape neck
Next row: Pat across 32(34,38) sts, turn and leave remaining sts on a spare needle.
Dec 1 st at neck edge on every row until 23(26,29) sts remain.
Work straight until front measures same as back to shoulders, ending with a wrong-side row.
Bind off.
Return to remaining sts.
With right side facing, slip first 11(13,13) sts onto a holder.
Join on yarn to remaining sts and pat to end.
Now complete to match first side of neck, reversing all shaping.

SLEEVES
Using smaller needles and A, cast on 37(41,43) sts.
Work 3(3,4)" in rib as for back, ending with rib row 1.
Inc row: Rib 5(4,5), ✭ M1, rib 3(3,2), rep from ✭ to last 5(4,4) sts, M1, rib to end: 47(53,61) sts.
Change to larger needles.
Work in pat as for back, increasing and working into pat 1 st each end of 5th and every following 4th(4th,6th) row until there are 67(79,83) sts.
Work straight until sleeve measures 8½(10, 12)", ending with a wrong-side row. Bind off loosely.

NECKBAND
Block the work.
Join shoulder seams.
With right side facing and using smaller needles and A, K across 12(12,13) sts from left back neck holder, pick up and K10(11,12) sts down left side of front neck, K across 11(13,13) sts from front neck holder, pick up and K10(11,12) sts up right side of front neck, then K across 12(12,13) sts from right back neck holder: 55(59,63) sts.
Beg with rib row 2, work 7 rows in rib.
Bind off in rib.

BUTTON BORDER
Using smaller needles and A, cast on 7 sts.
Rib row 1 (right side): K2, ✭ P1, K1, rep from ✭ to last st, K1.
Rib row 2: K1, ✭ P1, K1, rep from ✭ to end.
Rep these 2 rows until border, slightly stretched, fits up left back opening to top of neckband.
Bind off.
Sew on the border and mark the positions for 3 buttons, the top one ½" below the top of the border, the lower one ¾" from cast-on edge and the other halfway between these two.

BUTTONHOLE BORDER
With right side facing and using smaller needles and A, slip 5 sts from safety-pin onto a needle, then inc into first st, P3, inc into last st: 7 sts.
Now beg with rib row 1, work as for button band, working buttonholes opposite markers as follows:
Buttonhole row (right side): Rib 3, yo, P2 tog, rib to end.

TO FINISH
Sew on buttonhole border. Sew lower edge of button border in place behind buttonhole border, then sew on the buttons. Sew in the sleeves, then join side and sleeve seams.

INSTRUCTIONS FOR TEDDY'S PULLOVER

BACK
✭✭ Using smaller needles and A, cast on 55 sts.
Rib row 1: K1, ✭ P1, K1, rep from ✭ to end.
Rib row 2: P1, ✭ K1, P1, rep from ✭ to end.
Rep these 2 rows for 1¼", ending with rib row 1.
Inc row: Rib 8, ✭ M1, rib 13, rep from ✭ to last 8 sts, M1, rib to end: 59 sts.
Change to larger needles.
Joining on lengths of B as required, work in patt as follows:
Row1 (right side): K8A, ✭ MB in B, K13 A, rep from ✭ to last 9 sts, MB in B, K8 A.
Row 2: P with A.
Row 3: K with A.
Row 4: P with A.

Rows 5–8: Rep rows 3 and 4 twice.
Row 9: K1 A, ✶ MB in B, K13 A, rep from ✶ to last 2 sts, MB in B, K1 A.
Row 10: P with A.
Rows 11–16: Rep rows 3 and 4 three times.
These 16 rows form the pat. ★★
Divide for back neck opening
Next row: Pat across 27 sts, turn and leave remaining sts on a spare needle.
Keeping pat correct, continue on these sts until back measures 5" from beg, ending with a wrong-side row.
Next row: Bind off 17 sts, pat to end.
Break off yarn and leave remaining 10 sts on a holder.
Return to remaining sts.
With right side facing, slip first 5 sts onto a safety-pin, join yarn to remaining sts, pat to end.
Now complete to match first side of neck, reversing all shaping.

FRONT
Work as for back from ★★ to ★★.
Continue in pat until front measures 3½" from beg, ending with a wrong-side row.
Shape neck
Next row: Pat across 23 sts, turn and leave remaining sts on a spare needle.
Dec 1 st at neck edge on every row until 17 sts remain.
Work straight until front measures same as back to shoulders, ending with a wrong-side row.
Bind off.
Return to remaining sts.
With right side facing, slip first 13 sts onto a holder, join on yarn to remaining sts and pat to end.
Now complete to match first side of neck, reversing all shaping.

SLEEVES
Using smaller needles and A, cast on 35 sts.
Work 2½" in rib as for back, ending with rib row 1.
Inc row: Rib 4, ✶ M1, rib 3, rep from ✶ to last 4 sts, M1, rib to end: 45 sts.
Change to larger needles.
Work in pat as for back until sleeve measures 5", ending with a wrong-side row.
Bind off loosely.

NECKBAND
Block the work.
Join shoulder seams.
With right side facing and using smaller needles and A, K across 10 sts from left back neck holder, pick up and K10 sts down left side of front neck, K across 13 sts from front neck holder, pick up and K10 sts up right side of front neck, then K across 10 sts from right back neck holder: 53 sts.

Beg with rib row 2, work 5 rows in rib.
Bind off in rib.

BUTTON BORDER
Using smaller needles and A, cast on 7 sts.
Rib row 1 (right side): K2, ✶ P1, K1, rep from ✶ to last st, K1.
Rib row 2: K1, ✶ P1, K1, rep from ✶ to end.
Rep these 2 rows until border, slightly stretched, fits up left back opening to top of neckband.
Bind off.
Sew on the border and mark the positions for 3 buttons, the top one ½" below the top of the border, the lower one ¾" from cast-on edge and the other halfway between these two.

BUTTONHOLE BORDER
With right side facing and using smaller needles and A, slip 5 sts from safety-pin onto a needle, then inc into first st, P3, inc into last st: 7 sts.
Now beg with rib row 1, work as for button border, working buttonholes opposite markers as follows:
Buttonhole row (right side): Rib 3, yo, P2 tog, rib to end.

TO FINISH
Sew on buttonhole border.
Sew lower edge of button border in place behind buttonhole border, then sew on the buttons.
Sew in the sleeves.
Join side and sleeve seams.

*"Happy Birthday to you,
Happy Birthday to you,
Happy Birthday dear Teddy,
Happy Birthday to you."*

SUNDAY BEST

A very smart double-breasted Aran jacket with a grown-up-looking roll collar.

MEASUREMENTS

To fit 18–20(20–22)" chest
Actual measurements 25(27)"
Length from shoulder 13(15)"
Sleeve seam 8½(10½)" (with cuff turned back)

MATERIALS

15(16) oz [400(450) g] of fisherman yarn
A pair each of size 3 and size 5 knitting needles
Cable needle
6 buttons and a stitch holder

GAUGE

20 sts and 26 rows to 4" measured over st st worked on larger needles

To save time, take time to check gauge.

SPECIAL ABBREVIATIONS

C2F, Cross 2 Front worked as follows: slip next stitch onto cable needle and leave at front of work, P1, then K1 from cable needle.
C2B, Cross 2 Back worked as follows: slip next stitch onto cable needle and leave at back of work, K1, then P1 from cable needle.
MB, Make Bobble as follows: all into next stitch work [K1, P1, K1 and P1], turn and P4, turn and K4, turn and P2 tog twice, then turn and K2 tog.
C4B, Cable 4 Back worked as follows: slip next 2 stitches onto cable needle and leave at back of work, K2, then K2 from cable needle.
C4F, Cable 4 Front worked as follows: slip next 2 stitches onto cable needle and leave at front of work, K2, then K2 from cable needle.

FLOWER STITCH PATTERN

17 sts
Row 1 (right side): P6, C2B, K1, C2F, P6.
Row 2: K5, C2F, K1, P1, K1, C2B, K5.
Row 3: P4, C2B, P2, K1, P2, C2F, P4.
Row 4: K3, C2F, K3, P1, K3, C2B, K3.
Row 5: P2, C2B, P4, K1, P4, C2F, P2.
Row 6: K2, P1, K5, P1, K5, P1, K2.
Row 7: P2, MB, P5, K1, P5, MB, P2.
Row 8: K8, P1, K8.
Row 9: P8, MB, P8.
Row 10: K17.
Row 11: P17.
Row 12: K17.
Row 13: P17.
Row 14: K8, P1, K8.
These 14 rows form the Flower stitch pat.

 The flower stitch and bobbles in this design are traditional features of Aran knitting. Combined with the double-breasted front and roll collar, they make an unusual and original little jacket – smart enough for Sunday best!

HONEYCOMB STITCH PATTERN

16(24) sts
Row 1 (right side): [C4B, C4F] 2(3) times.
Row 2 and every other row: P16(24).
Row 3: K16(24).
Row 5: [C4F, C4B] 2(3) times.
Row 7: K16(24).
Row 8: P16(24).
These 8 rows form the Honeycomb stitch pat.

BACK

Using smaller needles cast on 63(71) sts.
Rib row 1: K1, * P1, K1, rep from * to end.
Rib row 2: K2, * P1, K1, rep from * to last st, K1.
Rep these 2 rows for 1½", ending with rib row 2.
Inc row: Rib 8, * inc in next st, rib 11(13), rep from * to last 7 sts, inc in next st, rib to end: 68(76) sts.
Change to larger needles.
Next row (wrong side): K1, P3, work [K8, P1, K8] to set flower pat, P3, K2, work P16(24) to set honeycomb pat, K2, P3, work [K8, P1, K8] to set flower pat, P3, K1.
Now work in pat as follows:
Row 1 (right side): K2, P1, K2, [P6, C2B, K1, C2F, P6] for first row of flower pat, K1, P1, K1, P2, [C4B, C4F] 2(3) times for first row of honeycomb pat, P2, K1, P1, K1, [P6, C2B, K1, C2F, P6] for first row of flower pat, K1, P1, K2.
Row 2: K1, P3, [K5, C2F, K1, P1, K1, C2B, K5] for second row of flower pat, P3, K2, P16(24) for second row of honeycomb pat, K2, P3, [K5, C2F, K1, P1, K1, C2B, K5] for second row of flower pat, P3, K1.
These 2 rows set position for flower and honeycomb pats.
Repeating rows 1 and 2 for borders in between pattern panels, continue in pat until back measures approximately 13(15)" from beg, ending with row 14 of flower pat.
Next row: Bind off 25 sts, pat until there are 18(26) sts on the needle, then bind off remaining 25 sts.

FRONTS (both alike)

Using smaller needles cast on 23 sts.
Work 1½" in rib as for back, ending with rib row 1, increasing 1 st each end of last row: 25 sts.
Change to larger needles.
Next row (wrong side): K1, P3, work [K8, P1, K8] to set flower pat, P3, K1.
Work in pat as follows:
Row 1 (right side): K2, P1, K1, [P6, C2B, K1, C2F, P6] for flower pat, K1, P1, K2.
Continue in pat as set until front measures the same as back to shoulders, ending with row 14 of the flower pat.
Bind off.

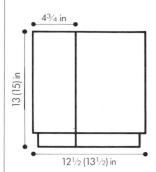

4³/₄ in

13 (15) in

12½ (13½) in

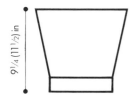

9¼ (11½) in

SLEEVES

Using smaller needles cast on 37 sts.
Work 1½(2)" in rib as for back ending with rib row 2.
Inc row: Rib 6, ✶ inc in next st, rib 3, rep from ✶ to last 7 sts, inc in next st, rib to end: 44 sts.
Change to larger needles.
Next row (wrong side): K5, P3, K2, P24 to set honeycomb pat, K2, P3, K5.
Work in pat as follows:
Row 1 (right side): K1, P4, K1, P1, K1, P2, (C4B, C4F) 3 times for honeycomb pat, P2, K1, P1, K1, P4, K1.
Row 2: K5, P3, K2, P24 for honeycomb pat, K2, P3, K5.
These 2 rows set pat. Continue in pat increasing and working into rev st st 1 st each end of 5th and every following 4th row until there are 54(64) sts.
Work straight until sleeve measures approximately 8½(10½)" with cuff turned back, ending with a wrong-side row.
Bind off.

COLLAR

Block the work.
Button band (left for a girl or right for a boy)
Join shoulder seams.
With right side facing and using smaller needles, pick up and K85(99) sts along front edge and K13 sts from back neck sts on holder (leaving remaining sts for buttonhole band): 98(112) sts.
Work 4(5)" in K1, P1 rib.
Bind off in rib.
Mark positions for 3 pairs of buttons, the first pair 1¼" from lower edge and 1" in from each side, then the other 2 pairs at 3" intervals.
Buttonhole band
Work as for button band, working buttonholes when ribbing measures 1" and 3" to correspond with markers as follows:
Buttonhole row (right side): Rib to position for first buttonhole, ending with a P1, ✶ K2 tog, yo, rib to next position for buttonhole, rep from ✶ once more, K2 tog, yo, rib to end.

TO FINISH

Join collar at center back neck. Fold sleeves in half lengthwise, then placing fold at top of sleeves at shoulder seams, sew in sleeves. Join side and sleeve seams. Sew on buttons.

BOLERO BELLE

A charming party-time wrap.

MEASUREMENTS

To fit 18–20(20–22)" chest
Actual measurements 20½(22)"
Length from shoulder 7¼(8¼)"; sleeve seam 3¼"

MATERIALS

2(3) oz (40[60] g) of an angora-blend yarn, such as Jaeger Angora Spun
A pair of size 5 knitting needles

GAUGE

25 sts and 33 rows to 4" measured over st st

To save time, take time to check gauge.

INSTRUCTIONS

RIGHT FRONT

Cast on 17(21) sts.

Shape front edge and work seed st border as follows:

Row 1: Inc into first st, [P1, K1] to end.

Row 2: [K1, P1] to last 2 sts, inc into next st, K1.

Rows 3–8: Rep rows 1 and 2 three times: 25(29) sts.

Row 9: Work in seed st over first 7 sts, inc into next st, K to end.

Row 10: K1, P to last 7 sts, seed st 7.

Rep rows 9 and 10 until there are 31(35) sts.

Keeping seed st border correct, continue in pat until front measures 3½(4½)" from beg, ending with a right-side row.

Shape for sleeve

Row 1: Cast on 7 sts, K1, P to last 7 sts, seed st 7: 38(42) sts.

Row 2: Seed st 7, K to end.

Rows 3 and 4: As rows 1 and 2: 45(49) sts.

Row 5: Cast on 7 sts, then seed st 7, P to last 7 sts, seed st 7: 52(56) sts.

Row 6: Seed st 7, K to last 7 sts, seed st 7.

Shape neck

Next row: Seed st 7, P to last 10 sts, P2 tog, P1, seed st 7.

Keeping seed st borders correct, work 3 rows straight.

Rep the last 4 rows until 45(49) sts remain.

Work straight until sleeve border measures 3¼" from beg of shaping.

Place a marker at each end of last row to denote shoulder line.

Work straight in pat for another 1", ending with a wrong-side row.

Break off yarn.

Leave sts on a spare needle.

Soft fluffy yarn guaran-tees that this classic bolero will continue to be a party-time favorite for years to come. Consider it an essential item in every well-dressed little girl's wardrobe!

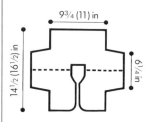

9¾ (11) in

14½ (16½) in

6¼ in

This little vest, with its two front pockets, is another classic design employing traditional techniques. There are instructions for both boys' and girls' buttoning.

LEFT FRONT

Cast on 17(21) sts.
Shape front edge and work seed st border as follows:
Row 1: [K1, P1] to last 3 sts, K1, P twice into next st, K1.
Row 2: Inc into first st, [K1, P1] to last st, K1.
Rows 3–8: Rep rows 1 and 2 three times: 25(29) sts.
Row 9: K to last 9 sts, inc into next st, K1, work in seed st to end.
Row 10: Seed st 7, P to last st, K1.
Rep rows 9 and 10 until there are 31(35) sts.
Keeping seed st border correct, continue in pat until front measures 3½(4½)" from beg, ending with a wrong-side row.

Shape for sleeve

Row 1: Cast on 7 sts, K to last 7 sts, seed st 7: 38(42) sts.
Row 2: Seed st 7, P to last st, K1.
Rows 3 and 4: As rows 1 and 2: 45(49) sts.
Row 5: Cast on 7 sts, then seed st 7, K to last 7 sts, seed st 7: 52(56) sts.
Row 6: Seed st 7, P to last 7 sts, seed st 7.

Shape neck

Next row: Seed st 7, K to last 10 sts, K2 tog, K1, seed st 7.
Keeping seed st borders correct, work 3 rows straight.
Rep the last 4 rows until 45(49) sts remain.
Work straight until sleeve border measures 3¼" from beg of shaping.
Place a marker at each end of last row to denote shoulder line.
Work straight in pat for another 1", ending with a wrong-side row.

Back

Next row: Pat across left front to last st, sl 1, turn and cast on 15 sts for back neck, turn and with right side facing, pat across sts of right front from spare needle: 105(113) sts.
Next row: Seed st 7, P31(35), seed st 29, P31(35), seed st 7.
Keeping seed st correct, work 6 more rows.
Next row: Seed st 7, K to last 7 sts, seed st 7.
Next row: Seed st 7, P to last 7 sts, seed st 7.
Rep these 2 rows until sleeve borders measure 6½" from beg, ending with a wrong-side row.

Shape sleeves

Bind off 7 sts at beg of next 6 rows: 63(71) sts.
Continuing in st st, work straight until back measures same as fronts from underarm to beg of seed st border, ending with a P row.
Next row: K1, [P1, K1] to end.
Rep this row 7 more times. Bind off purlwise.

TO FINISH

Block the work.
Join side and sleeve seams.

BIRTHDAY BOY

A smart vest with a clever cable rib.

MEASUREMENTS

To fit 20–22" chest
Actual measurements 23½"
Length from shoulder 13"

MATERIALS

6 oz [150 g] of a smooth, medium-weight yarn, such as Phildar Pronostic
A pair each of size 1 and size 3 knitting needles
Cable needle
Set of four size 1 double-pointed needles
2 stitch holders

GAUGE

24 sts and 32 rows to 4" measured over st st worked on larger needles

To save time, take time to check gauge.

SPECIAL ABBREVIATION

C4B, Cable 4 Back worked as follows: slip next 2 sts onto a cable needle and leave at back of work, K2, then K2 from cable needle.

INSTRUCTIONS

POCKET LININGS (make 2)

Using smaller pair of needles cast on 20 sts.
Work 2" st st, ending with a P row.
Break off yarn and leave sts on a spare needle.

BACK AND FRONTS

(Worked in one piece to armholes)
Using smaller pair of needles cast on 136 sts.
Work in cable rib as follows:
Row 1: K1, ✻ P2, K4, rep from ✻ to last 3 sts, P2, K1.
Row 2 and every other row: K3, ✻ P4, K2, rep from ✻ to last st, K1.
Row 3: As row 1.
Row 5: K1, ✻ P2, C4B, rep from ✻ to last 3 sts, P2, K1.
Row 7: As row 1.
Row 9: As row 1.
Row 11: As row 5.
Row 13: As row 1.
Row 14 (inc row): K3, P4, K2 to form the 9 border sts, K3, [inc in next st, K7] 4 times, inc into next st, K4, K2, P4, K2, K2 tog, K18, K2 tog, K2, P4, K2, K4, [inc into next st, K7] 4 times, inc into next st, K3, K2, P4, K3: 144 sts. Change to larger needles.
Now work in pat as follows:
Row 1 (right side): K1, P2, K4, P2 for border, P20 for pocket, [K1, P1] 12 times, K1 to form seed st, P2, K4, P2 for cable, P20 for pat panel, P2, K4, P2 for cable,

[K1, P1] 12 times, K1 for seed st, P20 for pocket, P2, K4, P2, K1 for border.

Row 2: K3, P4, K2 for border, [P3 tog, work (K1, P1 and K1) all into next st] 5 times for pocket, [K1, P1] 12 times, K1 for seed st, K2, P4, K2 for cable, [P3 tog, work (K1, P1 and K1) all into next st] 5 times for pat panel, K2, P4, K2 for cable, [K1, P1] 12 times, K1 for seed st, [P3 tog, work (K1, P1 and K1) all into next st] 5 times for pocket, K2, P4, K3 for border.

Row 3: K1, P2, C4B, P2 for border, P20 for pocket, seed st 25, P2, C4B, P2 for cable, P20 for pat panel, P2, C4B, P2 for cable, seed st 25, P20 for pocket, P2, C4B, P2, K1 for border.

Row 4: K3, P4, K2 for border, [work (K1, P1 and K1) all into next st, P3 tog] 5 times for pocket, seed st 25, cable 8, [work (K1, P1 and K1) all into next st, P3 tog] 5 times for pat panel, cable 8, seed st 25, [work (K1, P1 and K1) all into next st, P3 tog] 5 times for pocket, K2, P4, K3 for border.

These 4 rows form the bobble pat over pockets and center back panel.

Continue in pat as set, working cable twists (C4B) every 6 rows until work measures approximately 3½" from beg, ending with a wrong-side row.

Next row: Pat across 9 border sts, slip next 20 sts onto a holder then [K1, P1] 10 times across one pocket lining from spare needle, pat across 25 sts of seed st panel, work across cable and pat panels, then pat across 25 sts of seed st panel, slip next 20 sts onto a holder and [K1, P1] 10 times across second pocket lining from spare needle, work across 9 border sts to end: 144 sts.

Next row: Pat across 9 border sts, seed st across next 45 sts, cable 8, pat across center panel, cable 8, seed st across next 45 sts, work across 9 border sts to end.

Keeping pat correct as now set, continue in pat until work measures 7½" from beg, ending with a wrong-side row.

Divide for armholes
Next row: Pat across 36 sts, turn and leave remaining sts on a spare needle.
Next row: Bind off 3 sts, pat to end.

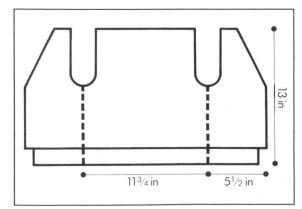

Next row: Pat 9, work 2 tog, pat to last 2 sts, work 2 tog.
Next row: Work 2 tog, pat to end.
Rep these 2 rows until 24 sts remain.
Next row: Pat 9, work 2 tog, pat to last 2 sts, work 2 tog.
Next row: Pat to end.
Rep these 2 rows until 16 sts remain.
Keeping armhole edge straight, continue to dec within the 9 st border on next and every other row until 10 sts remain.
Work straight until front measures 13" from beg, ending with a wrong-side row. Bind off.
Return to remaining sts.
With right side facing, join on yarn and pat across first 72 sts.
Bind off 3 sts at beg of next 2 rows.
Dec 1 st each end of following 7 rows, then dec 1 st each end of every other row until 46 sts remain.
Work straight until back measures 2 rows less than right front, ending with a wrong-side row.

Shape shoulders
Bind off 10 sts at beg of next 2 rows.
Break off yarn and leave remaining 26 sts on a holder.
Return to remaining sts.
With right side facing, rejoin yarn and bind off first 3 sts, pat to end.
Pat 1 row.
Next row: Work 2 tog, pat to last 11 sts, work 2 tog, pat to end.
Next row: Pat to last 2 sts, work 2 tog.
Rep these 2 rows until 24 sts remain.
Next row: Work 2 tog, pat to last 11 sts, work 2 tog, pat to end.
Next row: Pat to end.
Rep these 2 rows until 16 sts remain.
Now complete to match right front.

NECKBAND
Block the work.
Join shoulder seams.
With right side facing and using smaller needles, pick up and K106 sts evenly up right front to shoulder, P across 26 sts from back neck holder, then pick up and K106 sts evenly down left front: 238 sts.
Row 1: K to end.
Row 2: K1, ✳ P2, C4B, rep from ✳ to last 3 sts, P2, K1.
Row 3: K3, ✳ P4, K2, rep from ✳ to last st, K1.
Boy's vest
Row 4: K1, [P2, K4] 29 times, [P2, K2 tog, yo, K2 tog tbl] 10 times, P2, K1.
Row 5: K3, [P1, P twice into next loop, P1, K2] 10 times, [P4, K2] 29 times, K1.
Girl's vest
Row 4: K1, [P2, K2 tog, yo, K2 tog tbl] 10 times, [P2, K4] 29 times, P2, K1.

Row 5: K3, [P4, K2] 29 times, [P1, P twice into next loop, P1, K2] 10 times, K1.
Boy's or Girl's vest
Row 6: K1, P2, K4, rep from ✲✲ to last 3 sts, P2, K1.
Rows 7 and 8: As rows 3 and 2.
Bind off knitwise.

ARMBANDS
With right side facing, using set of 4 double-pointed needles and beg at underarm, pick up and K78 sts evenly around armhole.
Round 1: P to end.
Round 2: [K4, P2] to end.
Round 3: [C4B, P2] to end.
Rounds 4—8: Rep round 2 five times.
Round 9: As round 3.
Bind off knitwise.

POCKET TOPS
With right side facing and using smaller needles work across 20 sts from spare needles as follows:
Row 1: P2, [P twice into next st, P2] 6 times: 26 sts.
Row 2: K2, ✲ P4, K2, rep from ✲ to end.
Row 3: P2, ✲ C4B, P2, rep from ✲ to end.
Row 4: K2, ✲ P4, K2, rep from ✲ to end.
Row 5: P2, ✲ K4, P2, rep from ✲ to end.
Rows 6 and 7: As rows 4 and 5.
Row 8: As row 4.
Row 9: As row 3.
Bind off purlwise.

TO FINISH
Sew on buttons where required, using eyelet holes in cables as buttonholes.
Sew down ends of pocket tops.

BEST BEAU

A cute little bow tie that fastens at the back.

MATERIALS
Small amount of medium-weight chenille yarn
A pair of size 2 knitting needles
Size D crochet hook

INSTRUCTIONS

TO MAKE
Cast on 1 st.
Row 1: K into front and back of st: 2 sts.
Row 2: P into front and back of first st, P1: 3 sts.
Continue in st st until work measures 3" from beg.
Shape center of bow
Dec 1 st at beg of next 2 rows: 1 st.
Now inc 1 st at beg of next 2 rows: 3 sts.
Continue in st st until work measures 6" from beg.
Shape end
Dec 1 st at beg of next 2 rows: 1 st.
Break off yarn and fasten off.

CENTER BAND
Cast on 2 sts.
Beg with a K row work in st st for 2", ending with a P row.
Bind off.

TO FINISH
Using crochet hook, crochet a chain approximately 24" long. Fold bow by placing cast-on and bound-off points at center back and sew in place. Fold band over center of bow and sew at back. Knot crocheted chain over back of band and sew to back of bow with small stitches.

♥ This smart chenille bow tie makes a special-occasion outfit really special. The bow is sewn together to make it sturdy and fastens at the back of the neck with a length of crocheted chain.

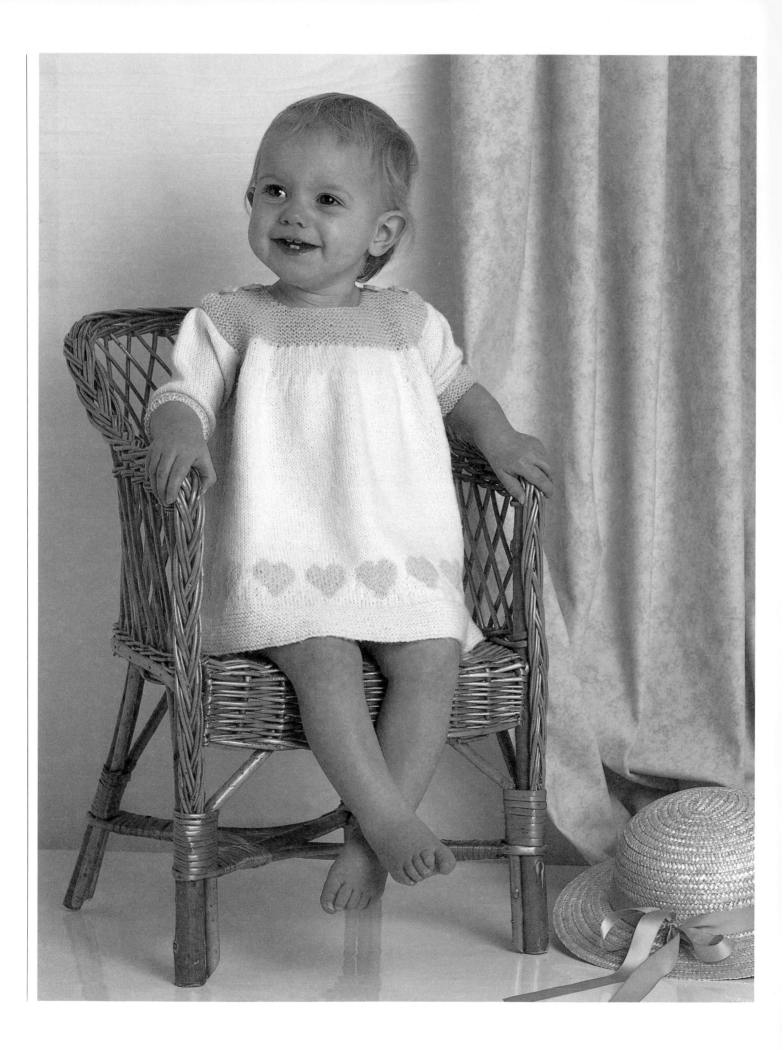

QUEEN OF HEARTS

Peach heart motifs make this simple little dress good enough for a special occasion!

MEASUREMENTS

To fit 16–18(18–20)" chest
Length from shoulder 13½(15¾)"
Sleeve seam 5(7)"

MATERIALS

4(6) oz [100(150) g] of a smooth fingering yarn, such as Pingouin Naturelle Fin, in main color A
2 oz [50 g] of same in contrasting color B
A pair each of size 0 and size 2 knitting needles
4 buttons

GAUGE

32 sts and 40 rows to 4" measured over st st worked on larger needles

To save time, take time to check gauge.

INSTRUCTIONS

FRONT

★ Using smaller needles and A, cast on 129 sts.
K 20 rows. Change to larger needles.
Beg with a K row, work 4 rows st st.
Work in pat, placing heart motifs from chart as follows:
Row 1: K8A, ★ 1B, 13 A, rep from ★ to last 9 sts, K1B, 8A.
Row 2: P7A, ★ 3B, 11A, rep from ★ to last 10 sts, P3B, 7A.
Continue in pat from chart until row 12 has been completed.
Using A only, continue in st st until front measures 10(11)" from beg, ending with a P row.
Shape armholes
Next row: Bind off 3 sts, then [K2, K2 tog] 30 times, K to end.
Next row: Bind off 3 sts, P to end: 93 sts.
Dec 1 st each end of next and every other row until

85 sts remain, ending with a P row.
Break off A and join on B.
Next row: ★ K1, K2 tog, rep from ★ to last st, K1: 57 sts. ★
K 20(30) rows.
Shape neck
Next row (wrong side): K19, bind off 19, K to end.
Working on first set of sts, K 13(17) rows.
Bind off.
Return to remaining sts.
Join on B and complete to match first side of neck.

BACK

Work as for front from ★ to ★.
K34(48) rows.
Bind off.

SLEEVES

Using larger needles and B, cast on 33(39) sts.
K 14 rows.
Break off B and join on A.
Work in rib as follows:
Rib row 1: K2, ★ P1, K1, rep from ★ to last st, K1.
Rib row 2: K1, ★ P1, K1, rep from ★ to end.
Rep these 2 rows 4 more times.
Inc row: ★ K3, M1, rep from ★ to last 3 sts, K3: 43(51) sts.
Beg with a P row, work 3 rows st st.
Continuing in st st, inc 1 st each end of next and every following 4th row until there are 61(77) sts.
Work straight until sleeve measures 6(8)" from beg, ending with a P row.
Shape top
Bind off 3 sts at beg of next 2 rows.
Dec 1 st each end of next and every other row until 47(63) sts remain, ending with a P row.
Bind off.

TO FINISH

Press or block, as appropriate for yarn used.
Join shoulder seams for about ¾" on each shoulder.
Make 2 button loops on each front shoulder.
Sew buttons to back shoulders opposite button loops.
Sew in sleeves. Join side and sleeve seams.

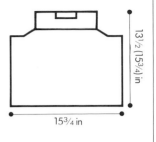

13½ (15¾) in

15¾ in

7½ (9½) in

6¾ (9) in

Knitted in a delicate fingering yarn, this pretty little hearts dress has three-quarter length sleeves with turn-back cuffs. The square neck has shoulder fastenings of buttons and button loops.

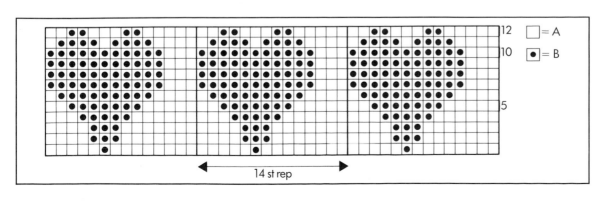

12

10

5

□ = A

●︎ = B

14 st rep

SEASHORE SPECIAL

Summer knitwear for babies and toddlers needs to be varied – cool enough to keep them comfortable in scorching weather, practical enough to withstand beach antics and frequent washing. Here, among other things, are cool white cotton knits, a pretty sundress and a traditional British Guernsey-style sweater for would-be fishermen ... and outfits for Teddy, too!

SHIP AHOY!

A sleeveless cotton top that can be worn either alone or over a T-shirt.

MEASUREMENTS

To fit 20(22)" chest
Actual measurements 22(24)"
Length from shoulder 11(12)"

MATERIALS

4 oz (100 g) of a lightweight cotton yarn, such as Phildar Perlé No 5, or Fil d'Ecosse in main color A
2 oz (50 g) of same in each of contrasting colors B and C
A pair each of size 1 and size 2 knitting needles
2 stitch holders

GAUGE

32 sts and 44 rows to 4" measured over st st worked on size 2 needles

To save time, take time to check gauge

INSTRUCTIONS

BACK

★ Using smaller needles and B, cast on 91(99) sts.
Rib row 1: K1, ★ P1, K1, rep from ★ to end.
Rib row 2: K2, ★ P1, K1, rep from ★ to last st, K1.
Rep these 2 rows for 1½", ending with rib row 2.

A little nautical nonsense with these charming seashore tops. They are knitted in fine cotton, which makes them light enough, by themselves, for hot weather or suitable to wear over a T-shirt. And, surprise, surprise, the boats reappear on the back!

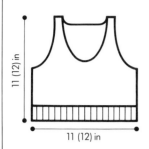

11 (12) in

11 (12) in

Change to larger needles.
Beg with a K row, work 4 rows st st.
Work motifs from chart as follows:

1st size only
Row 1: K1A, ✷ 4B, 2A, rep from ✷ to end.
Row 2: P3A, ✷ 2B, 4A, rep from ✷ to last 4 sts, K2B, 2A.

2nd size only
Row 1: K3B, ✷ 2A, 4B, rep from ✷ to end.
Row 2: P1A, ✷ 2B, 4A, rep from ✷ to last 2 sts, P2B.
Break off B.
Work 2 rows A.
Now continuing from chart, work as follows:
Row 5: K18(22)A, 12C, 12A, 12C, 12A, 12C, 13(17)A.
Row 6: P12(16)A, 20C, 4A, 20C, 4A, 20C, 11(15)A.
Continue in this way working from chart until row 34
has been completed.
Working in A only, continue in st st until back
measures 5½(6½)" from beg, ending with a P row.
Shape armholes
Next row: K5 and slip these sts onto a safety pin, K to
end.
Next row: P5 and slip these sts onto a safety pin, P to
end: 81(89) sts.
Dec 1 st each end of every row to 59(67) sts, then
every other row until 51(59) sts remain. ★
Work straight until back measures 10¼(11¼)" from
beg, ending with a P row.
Shape neck
Next row: K16(20), turn and leave remaining sts on a
spare needle. Dec 1 st at neck edge on every row
until 8(12) sts remain.
Now bind off.
Return to sts on spare needle.
With right side facing, slip first 19 sts onto a holder,
join yarn to next st and complete to match first side
of neck.

FRONT
Work as for back from ★ to ★.
Shape neck
Next row: K20(24), turn and leave remaining sts on a
spare needle.
Dec 1 st at neck edge on next and every other row
until 8(12) sts remain.
Work straight until front measures same as back to
shoulders.
Return to sts on spare needle.
With right side facing, slip first 11 sts onto a holder,
join yarn to next st and complete 2nd side of neck to
match first.

NECKBAND
Join right shoulder seam.
With right side facing, smaller needles and A, pick
up and K36 sts down left side of front neck, K across
11 sts from holder, pick up and K35 sts up right side
of neck and 7 sts down right back neck, K across 19
sts from holder, then pick up and K7 sts up left back
neck: 115 sts.
Beg with rib row 2, work 7 rows rib.
Bind off knitwise.

ARMHOLE BORDERS
Join left shoulder and neckband seam.
With right side facing, smaller needles and A, pick
up and K115 sts evenly around armhole, including
the 5 sts at each end on safety pins.
Beg with rib row 2, work 7 rows rib.
Bind off knitwise.

TO FINISH
Press or block, according to yarn used. Join side and
armhole border seams.

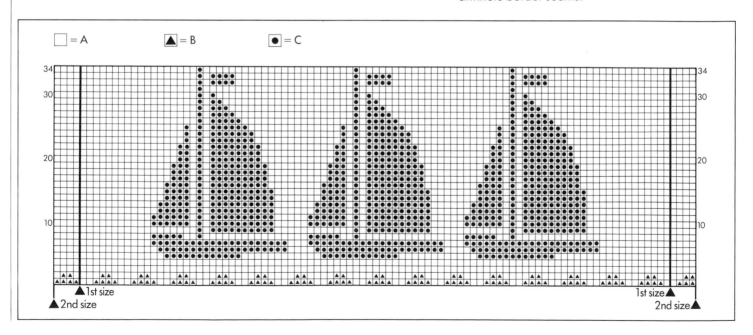

□ = A   ▲ = B   ⊙ = C

"I saw a ship a-sailing,
    A sailing on the sea,
And oh but it was laden
    With pretty things for thee.

There were comfits in the
    cabin,
    And apples in the hold;
The sails were made of silk,
    And the masts were all of
    gold.

The four-and-twenty sailors
    That stood between the
    decks,
Were four-and-twenty white
    mice
    With chains about their
    necks.

The captain was a duck
    With a pack upon his back,
And when the ship began to
    move,
    The captain said Quack!
    Quack!''

SAILOR STRIPS

A two-piece sailor suit consisting of square-necked T-shirt and Bermuda shorts.

MEASUREMENTS
Child's T-shirt
To fit 18(20,22)" chest
Actual measurements 20(22,24)"
Length from shoulder 10(11,12)"
Sleeve seam 3"
Child's shorts
To fit 20 to 22" waist
Waist to crotch 8"
Inside leg 6" (adjustable)
Teddy's T-shirt and shorts
To fit 15" chest
Height 19"

MATERIALS
Child's T-shirt
4 oz (100 g) of a lightweight cotton yarn, such as Phildar Perlé No 5 or Fil d'Ecosse, in main color A
2 oz (50 g) of same in contrasting color B
Child's shorts
4 oz (100 g) of same in main color A
2 oz (50 g) of same in contrasting color B
Waist length of elastic
Teddy's T-shirt
2 oz (50 g) of same in main color A
2 oz (50 g) of same in contrasting color B
Size B crochet hook and one button
Teddy's shorts
2 oz (50 g) of same in main color A
2 oz (50 g) of same in contrasting color B
Waist length of elastic
For all garments
A pair each of size 1 and size 2 knitting needles
A set of four double-pointed size 1 knitting needles or one size 1 circular needle 16" long

GAUGE
32 sts and 44 rows to 4" measured over st st worked on size 2 needles

To save time, take time to check gauge.

INSTRUCTIONS FOR CHILD'S T-SHIRT

BACK
★ Using smaller needles and A, cast on 83(91, 99) sts.
Rib row 1: K1, ★ P1, K1, rep from ★ to end.
Rib row 2: P1, ★ K1, P1, rep from ★ to end.
Rep these 2 rows for 1½", ending with rib row 2.
Change to larger needles.
Proceeding in st st, work in stripes of 2 rows A and 2 rows B until back measures 5½(6½,7½)" from beg,
ending with a P row.
Place a marker at each end of last row to denote beg of armhole. ★
Continue in st st stripes until back measures 9(10,11)" from beg, ending with a P row.
Shape back neck
Keeping stripe pat correct, K22(25,29) then turn and leave remaining sts on a spare needle.
Work straight for another 1", ending with a P row in A. Bind off.
Return to sts on spare needle.
With right side facing, slip first 41 sts onto a holder, then complete second side to match first.

FRONT
Work as for back from ★ to ★.
Continue in st st stripes until front measures 7(8,9)" from beg, ending with a P row.
Shape front neck
Keeping stripe pat correct, K22(25,29), then turn and leave remaining sts on a spare needle.
Work straight until front measures same as back to shoulders, ending with a P row.
Bind off.
Return to sts on spare needle.
With right side facing, slip first 41 sts onto a holder, then complete second side to match first.

SLEEVES
Join shoulder seams.
With right side facing and using larger needles and A, pick up and K75 sts between armhole markers.
P 1 row.
Beg with B, work in 2-row st st stripes until sleeve measures 2¼" from beg, ending with a P row.
Change to pair of smaller needles.
Beg with rib row 2 and using A, work 7 rows rib.
Bind off knitwise.

NECK
With right side facing, set of four double-pointed needles or circular needle and A, join yarn at neck on left shoulder and pick up and K24 sts down left front neck, K across 41 sts from holder, pick up and K24 sts up right side of front neck, 9 sts down right back neck, K across 41 sts from holder, then pick up and K9 sts up left back neck: 148 sts.
Working in rounds, K 1 round.
Now shape neck as follows:
Round 1 (dec round): [K1, P1] 10 times, K1, P2 tog, K corner st, P2 tog, [K1, P1] 18 times, K1, P2 tog, K corner st, P2 tog, [K1, P1] 13 times, K1, P2 tog, K corner st, P2 tog, [K1, P1] 18 times, K1, P2 tog, K corner st, P2 tog, [K1, P1] 3 times.
Round 2: Rib to end.
Work 5 more rounds in rib, working P2 tog each side of corner sts on next and every other row. Bind off purlwise.

 Delightful little cotton outfits – reminiscent of Victorian bathing suits – which are simple, practical and easy to wear. Substitute navy blue or red for the pale blue for a very different effect.

Dressing Teddy in his version of "Sailor Stripes" is child's play! His T-shirt has a single button at the back, making it easy to put on and take off.

TO FINISH

Press or block, as appropriate for yarn used. Join side and sleeve seams.

INSTRUCTIONS FOR CHILD'S SHORTS

RIGHT LEG

★ Using pair of smaller needles and A, cast on 85 sts.
Beg with a K row, work 10 rows st st.
Change to larger needles.
Work another 10 rows st st.
Fold work in half to wrong side and make hem as follows:
Next row: K1, pick up first loop from cast-on edge and K tog with next st on left-hand needle, ★ pick up next loop from cast-on edge and K tog with next st on left-hand needle, rep from ★ to end.
P 1 row.
Now working in stripes of 2 rows B and 2 rows A, continue straight in st st until leg measures 4" from lower edge (or desired length), ending with a P row.
Shape crotch
Inc 1 st each end of next and every following 3rd row until there are 101 sts.
Work 2 rows straight, so ending with a P row. ★
Shape back
Dec 1 st at end of next and every following 6th row until 88 sts remain.
Work 2 rows straight, so ending with a K row.

Breaking off yarn and rejoining as necessary, continue as follows:
Row 1: P to last 12 sts, turn.
Row 2 and every other row: K to end.
Row 3: P to last 20 sts, turn.
Row 5: P to last 28 sts, turn.
Row 7: P to last 36 sts, turn.
Row 9: P across all 88 sts.
Break off yarn and leave sts on a spare needle.

LEFT LEG

Work as for right leg from ★ to ★.
Shape back
Dec 1 st at beg of next and every following 6th row until 88 sts remain, so ending with a K row.
P 1 row.
Now continue as follows:
Row 1: K to last 12 sts, turn.
Row 2 and every other row: P to end.
Row 3: K to last 20 sts, turn.
Row 5: K to last 28 sts, turn.
Row 7: K to last 36 sts, turn.
Row 9: K across all 88 sts.
Row 10: P to end.
Do not break off yarn.

WAISTBAND

Next row: Using pair of smaller needles and A, K across the first 87 sts of left leg, then working across

sts of right leg, K tog the last st of left leg with first st of right leg, K across remaining 87 sts: 175 sts.
Beg with a P row, work another 20 rows st st.
Bind off.

TO FINISH
Press or block, as appropriate for yarn used. Join inside leg seams. Join front and back seams. Fold waistband in half to wrong side and slipstitch in place, leaving an opening for elastic. Thread elastic into casing and secure.

INSTRUCTIONS FOR TEDDY'S T-SHIRT

BACK
★ Using pair of smaller needles and A, cast on 65 sts.
Rep 6 rows in rib as for child's T-shirt, inc 1 st at end of last row: 66 sts.
Change to larger needles.
Working in stripes of 2 rows B and 2 rows A, continue in st st until back measures 3½" from beg, ending with a P row.
Place a marker at each end of last row to denote beg of armholes. ★

Divide for back opening
Next row: K33, turn and leave remaining sts on a spare needle.
Continue in st st stripes on these sts until back measures 6½" from beg, ending with a P row.

Shape neck
Next row: K17, turn and leave remaining sts on a holder.
Continue on these sts until work measures 7½" from beg, ending with a P row.
Bind off.
Return to sts on spare needle and complete to match first side, reversing shaping.

FRONT
Work as for back from ★ to ★.
Continue in stripes until front measures 5½" from beg, ending with a P row.

Shape neck
Next row: K17, turn and leave remaining sts on a spare needle.
Work straight on these sts until front measures same as back to shoulders, ending with a P row.
Bind off.
Return to sts on spare needle.
With right side facing, slip first 32 sts onto a holder, rejoin yarn to next st and complete to match first side of neck.

SLEEVES
Join shoulder seams.
With right side facing and using larger needles and A, pick up and K67 sts between armhole markers.
P 1 row.

Beg with B, work in 2-row st st stripes for 8 rows, ending with a P row.
Change to pair of smaller needles.
Beg with rib row 2 and using A, work 5 rows rib.
Bind off knitwise.

NECK
With right side facing, using pair of smaller needles and A, join yarn at back neck opening and K across 16 sts from holder, pick up and K25 sts up left back neck and down left front neck, K across 32 sts from holder, pick up and K26 sts up right side of front neck and down right back neck, then K across 16 sts from holder: 115 sts.
Working backward and forward in rows, work 5 rows in rib, dec 1 st each side of corner sts on next and every other row.
Bind off purlwise.

TO FINISH
Press or block, as appropriate for yarn used. Join side and sleeve seams. Using crochet hook and A, work 2 rows sc down left back opening and 4 rows down right back opening, making one 5 ch button loop at top on right back.
Sew on button. Slipstitch lower edges of opening neatly in place.

INSTRUCTIONS FOR TEDDY'S SHORTS

RIGHT LEG
Using pair of smaller needles and A, cast on 75 sts.
Beg with a K row, work 6 rows in st st; change to larger needles and work another 6 rows.
Make hem as for child's shorts.

Shape leg
Working in 2-row st st stripes, inc 1 st each end of 3rd and every other row until there are 81 sts.
Work 1 row.

Shape back
Dec 1 st at end of next and every other row until 67 sts remain.
Work straight until leg measures 5" from beg, ending with a P row.
Break off yarn and leave sts on a spare needle.

LEFT LEG
Work as for right leg, reversing all shaping, but do not break off yarn.

WAISTBAND
Next row: Using pair of smaller needles and A, K across the first 66 sts of left leg, then working across sts of right leg, K tog the last st of left leg with first st of right leg, K across remaining 66 sts: 133 sts.
Beg with a P row, work another 20 rows st st.
Bind off.
Complete as for child's shorts.

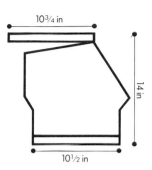
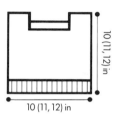
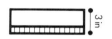

10¾ in
14 in
10½ in

10 (11, 12) in
10 (11, 12) in

3 in

SUN HAT

A tiny mob cap knitted in one from brim to crown.

MEASUREMENTS
Actual measurement around hat 14(16,18, 20)"
Depth 4(4¾,5,5½)"

MATERIALS
2(2,4,4) oz (50[50,100,100] g) of a lightweight cotton yarn, such as Phildar Perlé No 5 or Fil d'Ecosse
Shirring elastic
A pair each of size 0 and size 2 knitting needles

GAUGE
32 sts and 44 rows to 4" measured over st st worked on size 2 needles

To save time, take time to check gauge.

INSTRUCTIONS

BRIM
Using larger needles cast on 225(257,289,321) sts.
Row 1: K to end.
Row 2: K1, * yo, K2 tog, rep from * to end.
Rows 3 and 4: K to end.
These 4 rows form pat. Rep them 4 more times.
Next row: * K2 tog, rep from * to last st, K1:
113(129,145, 161) sts. Now K 1 row.

CROWN
Change to smaller needles.
Using shirring elastic together with yarn, work as follows:
Row 1: K1, * P1, K1, rep from * to end.
Row 2: K2, * P1, K1, rep from * to last st, K1.
Break off elastic.
Using yarn only, rep the last 2 rows three more times.
Change to larger needles.
Continue as follows:
* **Rows 1 to 3:** K to end.
Row 4: K1, * yo, K2 tog, rep from * to end.
Rows 5 and 6: K to end. *
Beg with a K row, continue in st st until work measures 4(4¾,5,5½)" from brim.
Rep the 6 rows from * to * once more. Now K 2 rows.
Shape crown
Row 1: * K2 tog, rep from * to last st, K1: 57(65, 73, 81) sts.
Row 2 and every other row: K to end.
Row 3: As row 1: 29(33,37,41) sts.
Row 5: As row 1: 15(17,19,21) sts.
Row 7: As row 1: 8(9,10,11) sts, break off yarn leaving a long length. Thread yarn through sts, draw up and fasten off securely. Join side seam.

HOLEY SUN TOP

A holey beach top with tiny cap sleeves, a square neck and shoulder fastening.

MEASUREMENTS
To fit 18" chest
Actual measurement 18"
Length from shoulder 11"

MATERIALS
4 oz (100 g) of a lightweight cotton yarn, such as Phildar Perlé No 5 or Fil d'Ecosse
A pair of size 2 knitting needles
2 buttons

GAUGE
24 sts to 4" measured over pattern

To save time, take time to check gauge.

INSTRUCTIONS

BACK
* Cast on 54 sts. K 6 rows.
Work in pat as follows:
Row 1 (right side): K to last st, sl last st.
Row 2: K1, * K2 tog, yo, rep from * to last st, K1.
Rows 3 to 5: K to last st, sl last st.
Row 6: K1, * yo, skpo, rep from * to last st, sl last st.
Rows 7 and 8: K to last st, sl last st.
These 8 rows form the pat.
Continue in pat until back measures 7" from beg, ending with a wrong-side row.
Shape armholes
Next row: Cast on 4 sts, K these 4 sts, then K to end of row.
Next row: Cast on 4 sts, K these 4 sts, then K1, pat to last 5 sts, K to end: 62 sts. *
Keeping the 5 sts at each end worked in g st, continue in pat until back measures 9½" from beg, ending with row 4 or 8 of pat.
** **Neck border**
Row 1: K to end.
Row 2: K5, pat across 10 sts, K32, pat across 10 sts, K5.
Rows 3 to 5: K to end.
Divide for neck
Next row: K5, pat across 10 sts, K5, bind off 22 sts, then K4, pat across 10 sts, K5.
Working on first set of sts, continue as follows:
K 3 rows.
Next row: K5, pat across 10 sts, K5. **
K 6 rows. Now bind off.
With right side facing, join yarn to remaining sts and complete to match first side of neck, ending with K 7 rows instead of 6. Now bind off.

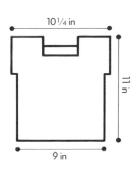

When "summer suns are glowing" this cotton sun hat will shade a little face, while the holey top will keep baby cool. Knitted in white, both look fresh and summery, but they would look just as cute in pale pastels.

FRONT

Work as for back from ★ to ★.

Keeping the 5 sts at each end worked in g st, continue in patt until back measures 8½" from beg, ending with a wrong-side row.

Now work neck border and shaping as for back from ★★ to ★★.

Continue in pat, keeping g st borders correct, until front measures same as back to beg of top border, ending with a wrong-side row.

K 8 rows.

Next row (buttonhole row): K5, yo, K2 tog, K to last 7 sts, K2 tog, yo, K5.

K 2 rows.

Bind off.

With right side facing, join yarn to remaining sts and complete to match first side, ending with K 6 rows instead of 8.

Bind off.

TO FINISH

Join right shoulder seam. Join side and underarm seams.

Sew on buttons opposite buttonholes.

BARNACLE BILL

A traditional Guernsey design — in miniature!

MEASUREMENTS

To fit 20(22)" chest
Actual measurement 24(26)"
Length from shoulder 12(13)"
Sleeve seam 9(10)"

MATERIALS

9(11) oz (250[300] g) of a smooth medium-weight yarn, such as Emu Guernsey 5 ply or No. 4 d'Anny Blatt
A pair of size 1 knitting needles
A set of four size 1 double-pointed needles
Stitch holder

GAUGE

32 sts and 44 rows to 4" measured over st st

To save time, take time to check gauge.

SPECIAL TECHNIQUE

Guernsey grafting Hold the wrong sides of work together, with the points of the needles holding the stitches both pointing the same way. Using a spare needle slip 1 st from each needle in turn onto the third needle until all stitches needed for grafting are on one needle, then bind off as follows:
[K2 tog] twice, pass the first st on right-hand needle over the second to bind it off, K the next 2 sts tog, then pass the first st on right-hand needle over the second again to bind it off. Continue in this way until all the stitches are bound off.

INSTRUCTIONS

BACK

Using pair of needles cast on 90(102) sts.
Work 16 rows g st. Work in rib as follows:
Rib row 1: K1, P1, K2, * P2, K2, rep from * to last 2 sts, P1, K1.
Rib row 2: * K2, P2, rep from * to last 2 sts, K2.
Rep these 2 rows twice more, then rib row 1 again.
Next row (right side): K15(21), * inc in next st, K9(14), rep from * to last 15(21)sts, inc in next st, K to end: 97(107) sts. **Next row:** K1, P to last st, K1.
Always working K1 at each end of every P row, continue in st st until work measures 7(8)" from beg, ending with a P row. Place a marker at each end of last row to denote beg of armhole. Work as follows:
Row 1: K6, P6, K to last 12 sts, P6, K6.
Row 2: K1, P to last st, K1.
Rep these 2 rows until work measures 12(13)" from beg, ending with row 2. Cut off yarn; leave sts on spare needle.

FRONT

Work as for back.

NECK GUSSETS

Holding wrong sides of back and front together, slip the first 22(27) sts from each needle onto spare needles for first shoulder seam, and join together using the Guernsey grafting technique; do not fasten off but leave the last st on a spare needle for the neck gusset.
Slip 53 neck sts at center of each piece onto spare needles, with points toward the grafted shoulder seam.
Using the needle with 1 st from shoulder grafting, K1 from the front needle holding 53 sts: 2 sts on right-hand needle. Turn.
Next row: Sl the first st, P1, then P1 from second set of 53 sts: 3 sts on right-hand needle. Turn.
Next row: Sl 1, then K2, K1 from first set of sts: 4 sts. Turn.
Continue in this way, working across 1 more st each time until there are 11 sts on the needle.
Break yarn and leave these sts on a holder.
Graft the 2nd set of 22(27) shoulder sts and work neck gusset in same way as first.

NECKBAND

Using the set of double-pointed needles, work 7 rounds in K2, P2 rib over all 108 sts on holders at neck.
Bind off purlwise.

SLEEVES

Using pair of needles cast on 54 sts.
Rib row 1: * K2, P2, rep from * to last 2 sts, K2.
Rib row 2: K1, P1, K2, * P2, K2, rep from * to last 2 sts, P1, K1.
Rep these 2 rows for 2(2½)", ending with rib row 2.
Work in st st, inc 1 st each end of next and every following 4th row until there are 82 sts.
Work straight until sleeve measures 8½(9½)" from beg, ending with a P row.
Work 7 rows in rib as for cuff.
Bind off knitwise.

UNDERARM GUSSETS

Using pair of needles cast on 1 st.
Working in st st, inc 1 st at beg of every row until there are 13 sts, then dec 1 st at beg of every row until 1 st remains.
Fasten off.

TO FINISH

Press or block, as appropriate for yarn used. Sew in sleeves between markers, then sew in underarm gussets.
Leaving lower edges open below ribbing, join side and sleeve seams.

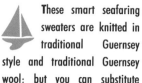 These smart seafaring sweaters are knitted in traditional Guernsey style and traditional Guernsey wool; but you can substitute another yarn of the same weight if you prefer.

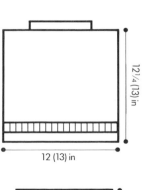

12¼ (13) in

12 (13) in

9 (10) in

BEACH BABY

Easy-fitting beach pants with bib.

MEASUREMENTS
To fit 18(20)" waist
Waist to crotch 8(9)"

MATERIALS
4 oz (100 g) of a medium-weight bouclé yarn, such as Phildar Skate
A pair each of size 2 and size 3 knitting needles
2 buttons
Waist length of elastic

GAUGE
22 sts and 32 rows to 4" measured over st st worked on size 3 needles

To save time, take time to check gauge.

INSTRUCTIONS

FRONT
(starting at bib)
Using larger needles cast on 25(29) sts.
Seed st row: K1, * P1, K1, rep from * to end.
Repeating this row forms the seed st pat.
Work 1 more row in seed st.
Next row (buttonhole row): K1, P1, yo, K2 tog, seed st to last 4 sts, K2 tog, yo, P1, K1.
Work 3 more rows in seed st.
Next row: Seed st 5, K15(19), seed st 5.
Next row: Seed st 5, P15(19), seed st 5.
Rep the last 2 rows until bib measures 4(4½)" from beg, ending with a wrong-side row.
Change to smaller needles.
Next row: Cast on 14 sts, [K1, P1] to last st, K1.
Next row: Cast on 14 sts, [K1, P1] to last st, K1: 53(57)sts.
** Now work rib casing for elastic as follows:
Row 1: * K1, yfwd, sl 1 pw, ybk, rep from * to last st, K1.
Row 2: K1, * K1, yfwd, sl 1 pw, ybk, rep from * to last 2 sts, K2.
Rep these 2 rows 3 more times. Change to larger needles.
Beg with a K row, work in st st until front measures 5(6)" from beg of rib casing, ending with a K row.
Divide for legs
Row 1 (wrong side): K1, P16(17), turn and leave remaining sts on a spare needle.
Row 2: K3, K2 tog, K to end.
Row 3: K1, P10(11), P2 tog, K3.
Row 4: As row 2.
Continue dec 1 st inside g st border in this way until 1 st remains.

Fasten off.
Return to sts on spare needle.
With wrong side facing, join yarn to first st, P to last st, K1.
Continue as follows:
Row 1: K12(13), K2 tog, K3, turn and leave remaining sts on a spare needle.
Row 2: K3, P2 tog, P to last st, K1.
Row 3: K10(11), K2 tog, K3.
Row 4: As row 2.
Continue dec 1 st inside g st border in this way until 1 st remains. Fasten off.
Return to sts on spare needle.
With right side facing, join yarn to first st and continue as follows:
Row 1: K to end.
Row 2: K3, P to last 3 sts, K3.
Rep these 2 rows 4 more times.
Still working 3 sts in g st at each end of the row, inc 1 st at each end of every row until there are 53(57)sts, ending with a wrong-side row.
Place a marker at each end of last row to denote end of front leg shaping.
Now continue with back as follows:
Beg with a K row, work in st st until back measures same as front from markers to beg of rib casing, ending with a P row.
Change to smaller needles.
Now work rib casing for elastic as follows:
Row 1: * K1, yfwd, sl 1 pw, ybk, rep from * to last st, K1.
Row 2: K1, * K1, yfwd, sl 1 pw, ybk, rep from * to last 2 sts, K2.
Rep these 2 rows 3 more times, then row 1 again.
Next row: K1, * P1, K1, rep from * to end. **
Divide for straps
With right side facing, bind off 12(14), then [P1, K1] 3 times, bind off 15, then [P1, K1] 3 times, bind off remaining 12(14) sts.
Using larger needles, join yarn to first set of 7 sts for strap and work in seed st until strap measures 10" from beg.
Shape end
Row 1: K2 tog, seed st to last 2 sts, K2 tog.
Row 2: Seed st to end.
Row 3: As row 1.
Bind off remaining 3 sts.
Work 2nd strap to match first.

TO FINISH
Join side seams, sew on buttons. Thread elastic (if required) through each section of casing and secure at each end.

Bright seashore colors will flatter any bright-eyed beach baby. If the bib and straps on these beach pants seem over-stretchy, they can be reinforced with a fabric or ribbon lining for extra strength.

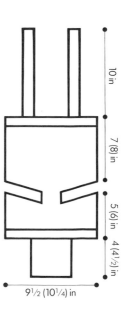

"Dance to your daddy,
My little babby,
Dance to your daddy,
My little lamb.

You shall have a fishy,
In a little dishy,
You shall have a fishy,
When the boat comes in."

BOTTOMS UP!

A version of the beach pants but without the bib.

MEASUREMENTS
To fit 18(20)" waist
Waist to crotch 8(9)"

MATERIALS
4 oz (100 g) of a medium-weight bouclé yarn, such as Phildar Skate
A pair each of size 2 and size 3 knitting needles
Waist length of elastic

GAUGE
22 sts and 32 rows to 4" measured over st st worked on size 3 needles
To save time, take time to check gauge.

INSTRUCTIONS

FRONT
Using smaller needles cast on 53(57) sts.
Rib row 1: K1, ✶ P1, K1, rep from ✶ to end.
Rib row 2: P1, ✶ K1, P1, rep from ✶ to end.
Now work as for Beach Baby bibbed pants on page 84, from ★★ to ★★ .

TO FINISH
Join side seams.
Thread elastic (if required) through each section of casing and secure at each end.

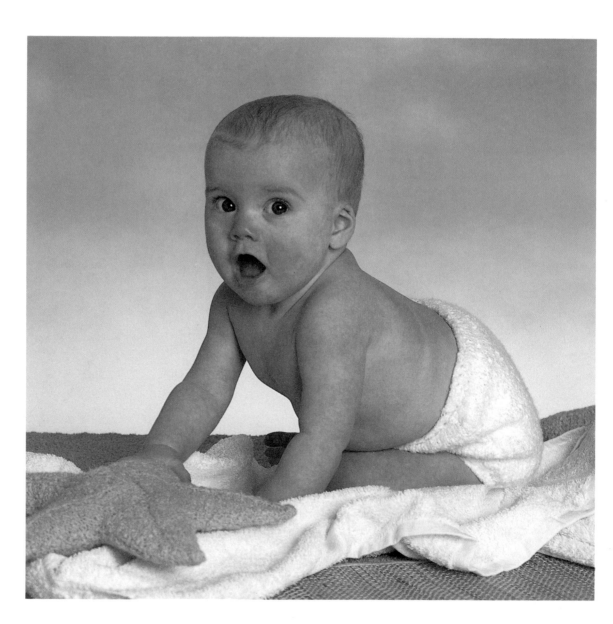

STELLA STARFISH

The starfish's points are knitted separately, then picked up on double-pointed needles and worked in rounds.

MEASUREMENTS

Actual measurements approximately 10(16)" in diameter

MATERIALS

2(4) oz (50[100] g) of a medium-weight bouclé yarn, such as Phildar Skate
A pair of size 3 and a set of four size 3 double-pointed knitting needles for the small starfish
A pair of size 7 and a set of four size 7 double-pointed knitting needles for the large starfish
Foam chips for stuffing

GAUGE

22 sts and 32 rows to 4" measured over st st worked on size 3 needles using 1 strand of yarn

To save time, take time to check gauge.

NOTE

The small starfish is knitted using 1 strand of yarn and the size 3 needles throughout, and the larger starfish is knitted to the same pattern using 2 strands of yarn together and the size 7 needles throughout.

INSTRUCTIONS

UNDERSIDE

* Using the smaller needles and 1 strand of yarn for the small star or the larger needles and 2 strands of yarn for the large star, cast on 3 sts.
Working in rev st st throughout, inc 1 st at each end of the 5th and every following 4th row until there are 13 sts.
Work 9 rows straight.
Work should measure 4(6)".
Break off yarn and leave sts on a spare needle.
Make 4 more pieces in the same way, but do not break off yarn on last piece.
Next row: P across 13 sts on needle, then P across 13 sts of each of the other 4 pieces: 65 sts.
Next row: K to end. *
Arrange sts onto three of the set of four double-pointed needles and work in rounds as follows:
Round 1: P4, P2 tog, * P11, P2 tog, rep from * to last 7 sts, P7: 60 sts.
Round 2 and every other round: P to end.
Round 3: P3, P2 tog, * P10, P2 tog, rep from * to last 7 sts, P7: 55 sts.
Continue dec in this way, working 1 st less between each dec, until 20 sts remain, and ending with a straight P round.

Next round: * P2 tog, rep from * to end: 10 sts.
Break off yarn, thread through sts and draw up tightly, then fasten off securely.

TOP SIDE

Keeping center st of each of the five points in st st (showing as a knit st on the right side) throughout, work as for underside from * to *.
Arrange sts on 3 of the set of four double-pointed needles and work in rounds as follows:
Round 1: P6, K1, P2 tog, * P10, K1, P2 tog, rep from * to last 4 sts, P4.
Round 2 and every other round: P all the purl sts and K all the knit sts to the end.
Round 3: P6, K1, P2 tog, * P9, K1, P2 tog, rep from * to last 3 sts, P3.
Continuing to dec after each K st in this way, complete as for underside.

TO FINISH

Placing right sides together, join outer edges, leaving a small section open for stuffing. Turn right side out, stuff firmly with foam chips and close opening securely.

Filled with foam chips – or chopped up (old!) pantyhose or stockings – this unusual knitted starfish is washable, chewable and virtually indestructible. What more could you ask for in a beach toy?

BEACH BELLE

The skirt and bodice of this sundress are one piece —
simply reduce the stitches by half at the waist!

MEASUREMENTS
To fit 18(20,22)" chest
Actual measurements 20(22,24)"
Length from shoulder 16(17,18)"

MATERIALS
6(8,8) oz (150[200,200] g) of a lightweight cotton
yarn, such as Phildar Perlé No 5 or Fil d'Ecosse in
main color A
2 oz (50 g) of same in contrasting color B (if motifs
desired)
A pair each of size 1 and size 2 knitting needles
Two short size 1 double-pointed knitting needles for
tubular knitting

GAUGE
32 sts and 44 rows to 4" measured over st st worked
on size 2 needles

To save time, take time to check gauge.

SPECIAL TECHNIQUE
Tubular Knitting Using double-pointed needles and
working over 5 sts, K 1 row.
Do not turn work but slip the 5 sts to the other end of
the needle, bring the yarn across the back of the
work and pulling yarn tightly K the row again from
right to left.
Continue in this way, always keeping the right side
of the fabric facing and always working from right to
left across the work, thus creating a tubular piece of
knitting.

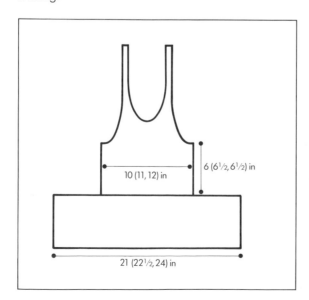

10 (11, 12) in

6 (6½, 6½) in

21 (22½, 24) in

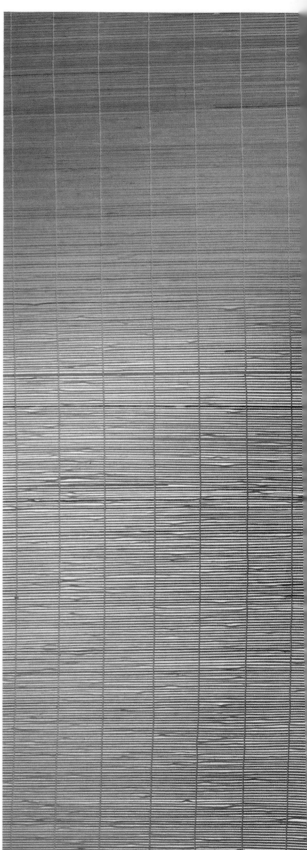

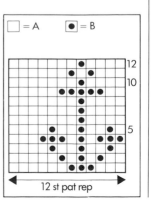

With or without the anchor motifs, these simple little sundresses are cool and comfy. They begin with a picot edge, the skirts are in stockinette stitch, the tops in reverse stockinette stitch and the ties in tubular knitting – what could be simpler?

☐ = A   ⦿ = B

12 st pat rep

INSTRUCTIONS

BACK AND FRONT (alike)
Using smaller needles and A, cast on
171(183,195) sts.
Beg with a K row, work 8 rows st st.
Next row: K1, ✳ yo, K2 tog, rep from ✳ to end.
Change to larger needles.
Beg with a P row, work 9 rows st st.
With wrong sides together, fold work along eyelet-
hole row and make hem as follows:
Next row: K1, pick up first loop from cast-on edge
and K tog with next st on left-hand needle, ✳ pick up
next loop from cast-on edge and K tog with the next
st on left-hand needle, rep from ✳ to end.
Work 3 rows st st.
Now working from chart, place motifs (if desired) as
follows:
Row 1: K6A, ✳ 3B, 9A rep from ✳ to last 9 sts, 3B, 6A.
Row 2: P5A, ✳ 1B, 1A, 1B, 1A, 1B, 7A, rep from ✳ to
last 10 sts, 1B, 1A, 1B, 1A, 1B, 5A.
Continue in this way working from chart until row 12
has been completed.
Break off B.
Using A only, continue in st st until skirt measures
5½(6,7)" (or desired length) from beg, ending with a
wrong-side row.
Dec row: K1, ✳ K2 tog, rep from ✳ to end:
86(92,98)sts.
Next row: K to end.
Beg with a P row, work in rev st st until bodice
measures 6(6½,6½)" from dec row, ending with a K
row.
✳ Shape armholes
Bind off 4 sts at beg of next 2 rows: 78(84,90) sts.
Dec 1 st each end of every row to 60(66,72) sts, then
at each end of every other row until 52(58,64) sts
remain, ending with a K row.
Work 2 rows straight.
Shape neck
Next row (right side): P21(24,26), bind off next
10(10,12) sts, P to end.
Working on first set of sts only, dec 1 st at neck edge
on next and every other row until 5 sts remain.
Work 1 row, then changing to double-pointed
needles, work 7(8,8)" of tubular knitting.
Break off yarn and thread through sts, draw up
tightly and fasten off securely.
Return to remaining sts.
With wrong side facing, join yarn to first st and
complete to match first side of neck.

TO FINISH
Join side seams.
Press skirt carefully if appropriate for yarn used.
Allowing neck and armhole edges to roll, tie straps
into a bow to fit. ✳

SUN TOP

This cute little sun top is created by omitting the skirt
from the sundress.

MEASUREMENTS
To fit 18(20,22)" chest
Actual measurements 20(22,24)"
Length from shoulder 10(11,12)"

MATERIALS
4 oz (100 g) of a lightweight cotton yarn, such as
Phildar Perlé No 5 or Fil d'Ecosse
A pair each of size 1 and size 2 knitting needles
Two short size 1 double-pointed knitting needles

GAUGE
32 sts and 44 rows to 4" measured over st st worked
on size 2 needles

To save time, take time to check gauge.

SPECIAL TECHNIQUE
Tubular knitting Using double-pointed needles and
working over 5 sts, K 1 row.
Do not turn work but slip the 5 sts to the other end of
the needle, bring the yarn across the back of the
work and pulling yarn tightly K the row again from
right to left. Continue in this way, always keeping the
right side of the fabric facing and always working
from right to left across the work, thus creating a
tubular piece of knitting.

INSTRUCTIONS

BACK AND FRONT (alike)
Using smaller needles cast on 85(91,97)sts.
Rib row 1: K1, ✳ P1, K1, rep from ✳ to end.
Rib row 2: K2, ✳ P1, K1, rep from ✳ to last st, K1.
Rep these 2 rows for 1", inc 1 st at end of last row:
86(92,98) sts.
Change to larger needles.
Beg with a P row, work in rev st st until top measures
4½(5½,6½)" from beg, ending with a K row.
Now complete as for the Beach Belle sundress from
✳ to ✳.

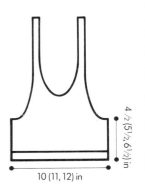

10 (11, 12) in

4½(5½,6½) in

Knitted in teddy bear shades of an angora-blend yarn, this furry pullover will enable any child to join the pack! If you knit this for a baby, a slightly brushed wool or wool-acrylic yarn might be more advisable, since angora yarns can be rather fluffy.

TEDDY BEARS

This chapter is devoted to bears. There are pullovers and overalls with teddy bear motifs, a family of three bears to knit, and garments inspired by teddy colors and textures. As everyone knows, children adore teddy bears; big or small, fat or thin, furry or fuzzy, they are the most popular of all soft toys. So, it's hardly surprising that in this section the bears take over!

FUZZY WUZZY

A long-sleeved pullover with a shirt-collar fastening and teddy bear motifs around the body.

MEASUREMENTS
To fit 18(20,22)" chest
Actual measurements 21(23,25)"
Length from shoulder 11(12,13)"
Sleeve seam 7(8,9)"

MATERIALS
2(2,3) oz [40(40,60) g] of a fine angora blend or wool-acrylic fingering yarn in main color A
1 oz [20 g] of same in contrasting color B
A pair each of size 0 and size 2 knitting needles
Stitch holder
3 buttons

GAUGE
34 sts and 47 rows to 4" measured over st st worked on larger needles

To save time, take time to check gauge.

INSTRUCTIONS

BACK
★ Using smaller needles and B, cast on 85(93,101) sts.
Rib row 1: K2, ★ P1, K1, rep from ★ to last st, K1.

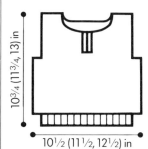
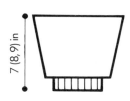

10³⁄₄ (11³⁄₄, 13) in

10½ (11½, 12½) in

7 (8,9) in

Rib row 2: K1, * P1, K1, rep from * to end.
Rep these 2 rows for 1¼(1¼,1½)", ending with rib row 2.
Change to larger needles. Break off B and join on A.
Inc row: K10(12, 13), * inc in next st, K12(13,14), rep from * to last 10(11,13) sts, inc in next st, K to end: 91(99,107) sts. P1 row. *
Beg with a K row, work in st st until back measures 6½(7,7½)" from beg, ending with a P row.

Shape armholes
Bind off 8 sts at beg of next 2 rows: 75(83,91) sts.
Work straight until back measures 10½(11½,12½)" from beg, ending with a P row.

Shape neck
Next row: K19(23,25), K2 tog, K2, turn and leave remaining sts on a spare needle.
Next row: P2, P2 tog, P to end.
Continue to dec 1 st in this way at neck edge until 17(21,23) sts remain, changing to B on the last row.
Using B, bind off. Return to remaining sts.
With right side facing, slip first 29(29,33) sts onto a holder, join yarn to remaining sts and complete to match first side of neck, reversing all shaping.

FRONT
Work as for back from * to * .
Beg with a K row, work 4 rows st st.
Using separate small balls of yarn for each Teddy motif, place motifs from chart as follows:
Row 1: K13(17,21)A, [5B, 7A] 5 times, 5B, 13(17,21)A.
Row 2: P12(16,20)A, [7B, 5A] 5 times, 7B, 12(16,20)A.
Continue in pat from chart until row 26 has been completed.
Working in A only, continue in st st until front measures same as back to armhole shaping, ending with a P row.

Shape armholes
Bind off 8 sts at beg of next 2 rows: 75(83,91) sts.
K1 row.

Divide for front opening
Next row: P34(38,42), turn and leave remaining sts on a spare needle.
Next row: Join on B and cast on 7 sts, [K1, P1] 3 times, K1, for button border, change back to A and K to end: 41(45,49) sts.
Twisting yarns together at back of work when changing color, continue in st st with A and seed st with B until front measures 20 rows less than back to shoulders, ending at neck edge.

Shape neck
Next row: Seed st 7B, K5(5,7)A then slip these 12(12,14) sts onto a safety-pin, work across 2 sts, work 2 tog, work to end.
Continue dec 1 st at neck edge, within the 2 st border, on every row until 17(21,23) sts remain.
Work straight until front measures same as back to shoulders, working last row in B. Using B, bind off.
Mark the positions for 2 buttons on this border, the first one 7 rows from beg of button border, then allowing for the 3rd one to be on the neckband, place the other one halfway between the others.
Return to remaining sts.
With wrong side facing, join B to first st, P7B, join on A and P to end: 41(45,49) sts.
Next row: K34(38,42)A, seed st 7B.
Now complete to match first side, reversing all shaping and working buttonholes opposite markers as follows:
Buttonhole row (wrong side): With B, K1, P1, K1, yo, skpo, P1, K1, then with A K to end.

SLEEVES
Using smaller needles and B, cast on 45(49,53) sts.
Work 1¼(1¼,1½)" in rib as for back.

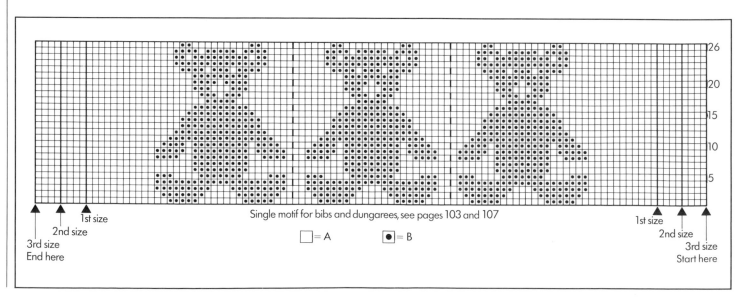

1st size
2nd size
3rd size
End here

Single motif for bibs and dungarees, see pages 103 and 107

□ = A   ⦿ = B

26
20
15
10
5

1st size
2nd size
3rd size
Start here

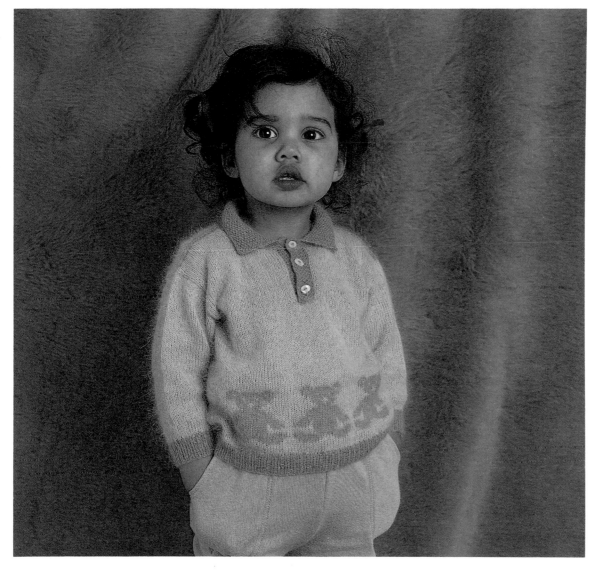

"Fuzzy Wuzzy was a bear,
A bear was Fuzzy Wuzzy.
When Fuzzy Wuzzy lost his
  fur,
He wasn't fuzzy, wuz he?"

Inc row: K1(3,4), ✳ inc in next st, K5, rep from ✳ to last 2(4,7) sts, inc in next st, K to end: 53(57,61) sts.
Change to larger needles. Break off B and join on A. Beg with a P row and working in st st, inc 1 st each end of 5th and every following 4th row until there are 75(83,91) sts.
Work straight until sleeve measures 7(8,9)" from beg.
Bind off.

NECKBAND AND COLLAR
(worked in one piece)
Join shoulder seams.
With right side facing and using smaller needles and B, seed st across 12(12,14) sts from safety-pin at right front, pick up and K18 sts up right side of front neck and 5 sts down right side of back neck, K across 29(29, 33) sts from back neck holder, pick up and K5 sts up left side of back neck and 18 sts down left side of front neck, then seed st across 12(12,14) sts from safety-pin at left front: 99(99,107) sts.
Next row: Seed st to end.
Next row: Seed st to last 4 sts, yo, skpo, P1, K1. Work 4 rows seed st.
Next row: Bind off 4 sts knitwise, seed st to end.
Next row: Bind off 4 sts purlwise, seed st to end: 91(91,99) sts.
Work 2" in seed st, ending with a right-side row.
Bind off knitwise.

TO FINISH
Press or block according to yarn used.
Fold sleeves in half lengthwise, then placing folds at shoulder seams, sew in sleeves.
Join side and sleeve seams.
Sew lower edge of button band neatly in place.
Sew on buttons opposite buttonholes.

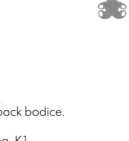

PLAYTIME

A high-waisted dress with a distinctive wide collar.

MEASUREMENTS

To fit 20(22,24)" chest
Length from shoulder 16(17¼,18½)"
Sleeve seam 10(10¼,10½)"

MATERIALS

9 oz [250 g] of a smooth, lightweight yarn, such as
Pingouin Pingofine, in main color A
4 oz [100 g] of a medium-weight bouclé yarn, such
as Phildar Skate, in contrasting color B
2 oz [50 g] of a smooth, medium-weight yarn, such
as Pingouine Confortable Fin, in contrasting color C
A pair each of size 0 and size 1 knitting needles
One size 1 circular needle, any length
Size C crochet hook; stitch holder

GAUGE

59 sts and 46 rows to 4" measured over rib worked
on larger needles with A
32 sts and 44 rows to 4" measured over st st worked
on larger needles with B

To save time, take time to check gauge.

INSTRUCTIONS

SKIRT

Using circular needle and A, cast on 404(440,476)
sts.
Working backward and forward in rows, work in K1,
P1 rib for 12 rows.
Continuing in rib, work 2 rows C, 22 rows A, 2 rows
B and 70(82,94) rows A.
Next row (dec row): ☆ K3 tog, rep from ☆ to last 2 sts,
K2 tog: 135(147,159) sts. Bind off.

BODICE AND SLEEVES

Using pair of larger needles and A, cast on 88 sts.
Work 24 rows in K2, P2 rib.
Inc row (right side): [K1, P1] into each st to end:
176 sts.
Now continuing in K1, P1 rib and inc 1 st each end of
next and every following 3rd row until there are
212 sts, work 3 rows A, 2 rows B, 22 rows A, 2 rows
C and 23 rows A.
Using A only, work 38(44,50) rows in rib.
Place a marker at each end of last row to denote
beg of bodice. Break off A and join on B.
Row 1 (wrong side): P4, ☆ P1, [P2 tog] 8 times, rep
from ☆ to last st, P4: 116 sts.
Beg with a K row, work 10 rows st st.
Divide for neck
Next row: K55, K2 tog, K1, turn and leave remaining

58 sts on a spare needle.
Continue on these 57 sts for back bodice.
Next row: P.
Next row: K to last 3 sts, K2 tog, K1.
Rep the last 2 rows twice more: 54 sts.
Work 74(86,96) rows st st.
Next row: K to last 2 sts, inc in next st, K1.
Next row: P.
Next row: K to last 2 sts, inc in next st, K1.
Rep the last 2 rows twice more: 58 sts.
Break off yarn and leave sts on a holder.
Return to sts on spare needle. With right side facing,
join on B, K1, K2 tog, K to end: 57 sts.
Next row: P.
Next row: K1, K2 tog, K to end of row.
Rep last 2 rows 4 more times: 52 sts.
Work 66(78,88) rows st st.
Next row: K1, inc in next st, K to end.
Next row: P.
Next row: K1, inc in next st, K to end.
Rep last 2 rows 4 more times: 58 sts.
Next row: P58 sts, then P across 58 sts from holder
116 sts.
Work 10 rows st st. Break off B and join on A.
Next row (inc row): K4, ☆ K1, [inc in next st] 8 times,
rep from ☆ to last 4 sts, K4: 212 sts.
Place a marker at each end of last row to denote
end of bodice.
Work 38(44,50) rows K1, P1 rib.
Continuing in rib and decreasing 1 st each end of
next and every following 3rd row until 176 sts
remain, work 23 rows A, 2 rows C, 22 rows A, 2 rows
B and 3 rows A.
Continuing in A only, work cuff as follows:
Next row: ☆ [K2 tog] twice, [P2 tog] twice, rep from ☆
to end: 88 sts. Work 24 rows K2, P2 rib.
Bind off in rib.

Bright colors make this
a stunning little play
dress. It's loose-fitting and has
long sleeves and an unusual wide
collar. The pattern for Teddy's
bib is on page 103.

9½ (10¼, 11½) in

14¼ in

9¾ (10¼, 10½) in

9 (10¼, 11½) in

26¾ (29, 31½) in

"If I was a bear,
And a big bear too,
I shouldn't much care
If it froze or snew;
I shouldn't much mind
If it snowed or friz–
I'd be all fur-lined
With a coat like his!"

COLLAR

With wrong side facing and using circular needle, join C to front neck approximately 2½" in from left shoulder, then pick up and K15(20,25) sts across to left shoulder, 50(67,72) sts across back neck, then 35(41,47) sts across front neck: 100(122,144) sts.
Inc row: Using A, P into back and front of next 2 sts, then using C, P into back and front of each st to end: 196(240,284) sts.
Always twisting A and C together when changing color, continue in rib as follows:
Rib row 1: With C, K4, ✿ P2, K2, rep from ✿ to last 6 sts, P2, then with A, K4.
Rib row 2: With A, P4, then with C, K2, ✿ P2, K2, rep from ✿ to last 6 sts, P2, K4.
Rep these 2 rows 16(17,18) more times. Bind off in rib.

TO FINISH

Press or block, as appropriate for yarn used.
Join center back skirt seam. Join sleeve seams to markers. Sew skirt to bodice. Sew button to left front collar edge.

INSTRUCTIONS FOR BAG

Using pair of larger needles cast on 5 sts in A, 20 sts in B and 5 sts in A: 30 sts.
Row 1: With A [K1, P1] twice, K1, with B, K20, with A [K1, P1] twice, K1.
Row 2: With A [P1, K1] twice, P1, with B, P20, with A [P1, K1] twice, P1.
Rep these 2 rows 41 more times. (84 rows altogether.)
Next row: In A only, [K1, P1] twice, K22, [P1, K1] twice.
Next row: In A only, [P1, K1] twice, P22, [K1, P1] twice.
Now rep rows 1 and 2 five more times.
Next row: In C only, [K1, P1] twice, K22, [P1, K1] twice.
Next row: In C only, [P1, K1] twice, P22, [K1, P1] twice.
Now rep rows 1 and 2 once.
Working in B only and st st, dec 1 st each end of next 7 rows: 16 sts.
Next row: P2 tog, P4, bind off 4 sts, P to last 2 sts, P2 tog.
Next row: K2 tog, K3, cast on 4 sts, K to last 2 sts, K2 tog.
Continue to dec 1 st each end of every row until 2 sts remain. Bind off.

TO FINISH

Press or block, as appropriate for yarn used.
Fold bag across width approximately 4" from cast-on edge and join side seams. Fold flap over at top and sew on button opposite buttonhole. Using A, crochet a chain to form strap to the length required. Sew strap to top of bag.

THE THREE BEARS

The Three Bears of storybook fame: Father Bear, Mother Bear and Baby Bear. Children will love these cuddly knitted toys.

MEASUREMENTS

Height approximately 12(16,20)"

MATERIALS

2(4,6) oz [50(100,150) g] of a smooth, lightweight yarn, such as Pingouin Pingofine
A pair of size 2 knitting needles for the small bear, size 5 for the medium bear and size 8 for the large bear
A small amount of black yarn for embroidering features
Washable stuffing

GAUGE

31 sts and 41 rows to 4" measured over st st worked on smallest needles using 1 strand
23 sts and 28 rows to 4" measured over st st worked on medium-size needles using 2 strands
18 sts and 22 rows to 4" measured over st st worked on largest needles using 3 strands

To save time, take time to check gauge.

NOTE

The pattern for all three bears is the same, the size being altered by using 1 strand of yarn for the small bear, 2 strands of yarn for the medium bear and 3 strands of yarn for the large bear.

INSTRUCTIONS FOR BEARS

BODY

Using the appropriate needles and number of strands of yarn (see note), cast on 32 sts. Beg with a K row work 32 rows st st.
Shape shoulders
Dec 1 st each end of every row until 18 sts remain. Work 1 row.
Shape face and nose
Row 1: Inc in first st, K7, M1, K2, M1, K7 inc into last st: 22 sts
Row 2 and every other row: P.
Row 3: Inc in first st, K9, M1, K2, M1, K9, inc in last st: 26 sts
Row 5: Inc in first st, K11, M1, K2, M1, K11, inc in last st: 30 sts
Row 7: Inc in first st, K13, M1, K2, M1, K13, inc in last st: 34 sts
Row 9: K16, M1, K2, M1, K16: 36 sts.
Row 11: K17, M1, K2, M1, K17: 38 sts.
Row 12: P.

Shape top of nose
Row 1: K17, K2 tog, K2 tog tbl, K17.
Row 2 and every other row: P.
Row 3: K16, K2 tog, K2 tog tbl, K16.
Row 5: K15, K2 tog, K2 tog tbl, K15.
Row 7: K14, K2 tog, K2 tog tbl, K14.
Row 9: K13, K2 tog, K2 tog tbl, K13.
Row 11: K12, K2 tog, K2 tog tbl, K12.
Row 12: P to end: 26 sts.

Shape top of head
Dec 1 st each end of next and every other row until 18 sts remain. Work 1 row.

Back of head
Inc 1 st each end of next and every other row until

there are 26 sts.
Work 15 rows straight, so ending with a P row.

Shape neck
Dec 1 st each end of next and every other row until 18 sts remain. Work 2 rows.

Shape shoulders
Inc 1 st each end of next 7 rows: 32 sts.
Back Work 32 rows straight.

Divide for legs
Next row: Cast on 16 sts, K these 16 sts, then K16, turn and leave remaining sts on a spare needle.
Work 38 rows st st on these 32 sts.

Sole
K 4 rows.

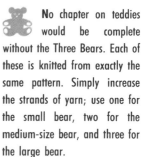 **No** chapter on teddies would be complete without the Three Bears. Each of these is knitted from exactly the same pattern. Simply increase the strands of yarn; use one for the small bear, two for the medium-size bear, and three for the large bear.

Shape sole
Next row: [K2 tog] 16 times.
K 3 rows.
Next row: [K2 tog] 8 times: 8 sts.
Break off yarn, leaving a long length, thread through sts, then draw up tightly and fasten off securely.
Return to remaining sts.
With right side facing, join on yarn and K16, turn and cast on 16 sts.
Now complete to match first leg.

ARMS

Using appropriate needles and number of strands of yarn, cast on 12 sts.
Beg with a K row and working in st st, inc 1 st each end of every row until there are 24 sts.
Work 32 rows straight.
Shape end of arms
K4 rows.
Next row: [K2 tog] 12 times.
K 3 rows.
Next row: [K2 tog] 6 times: 6 sts.
Break off yarn leaving a long length, thread through sts, then draw up tightly and fasten off securely.

EARS

Using appropriate needles and number of strands of yarn, cast on 6 sts.
Beg with a K row and working in st st, inc 1 st each end of every row until there are 14 sts.
Work 4 rows straight.
Dec 1 st each end of next and every other row until 8 sts remain, so ending with a K row.
K1 row to make a ridge on right side.
Continuing in st st, inc 1 st each end of every row until there are 14 sts.
Work 5 rows straight.
Dec 1 st each end of every row until 6 sts remain.
Bind off.

TO FINISH

Using black yarn, embroider eyes, nose and mouth following diagram above.
Join leg seams, then stuff firmly. Join lower edge of front body to tops of legs, then join body and head seams, leaving a small opening. Stuff body, head, and neck firmly, then close opening neatly. Join arm seams, stuff firmly, then sew to body at shoulders. Fold ears in half and join side seams, then sew in place.

Where else would you expect to find bears but in the woods? These particular bears are rather shy and only peep out from the trees. This makes them great favorites with toddlers, who love to spot them!

BEARS IN THE WOOD

A round-neck pullover with a tree and bear motif.

MEASUREMENTS

To fit 20(22)" chest
Actual measurements 25(27)"
Length from shoulder 14(15¾)"
Sleeve seam 9(10¼)"

MATERIALS

6(6,8) oz [150(150,200) g] of a smooth, lightweight yarn, such as Patons Diploma 4 ply, in main color A
2(2,4) oz [50(50,100) g] of same in contrasting color B
2 oz [50 g] of same in each of contrasting colors C, D and E
A pair each of size 2 and size 3 knitting needles
3 buttons; 2 stitch holders

GAUGE

28 sts and 36 rows to 4" measured over st st worked on larger needles

To save time, take time to check gauge.

INSTRUCTIONS

BACK

Using smaller needles and A, cast on 69(77) sts.
Rib row 1: K1, * P1, K1, rep from * to end.
Rib row 2: P1, * K1, P1, rep from * to end.
Rep these 2 rows for 2", ending with rib row 1.
Inc row: Rib 6(5), * M1, rib 3, M1, rib 3(4), rep from * to last 3(2) sts, rib to end: 89(97) sts.
Change to larger needles.
Beg with a K row, work 4 rows st st.
Using separate balls of yarn for each motif and twisting yarns together at back of work when changing color to avoid making a hole, place first and 2nd motifs as follows:
Row 1: K3(5)A, working from chart [K10A, 5C, 10A], K33(37)A, working from chart [K10A, 5C, 10A], then K3(5)A.
Row 2: P3(5)A, working from chart [P10A, 5C, 10A], P33(37)A, working from chart [P10A, 5C, 10A], then P3(5)A.
Continue working motifs from chart as established until row 18 has been completed.
Now continuing to work motifs as set, place 3rd motif in between first two as follows:
Next row: K3(5)A, pat across row 19 of chart, K4(6)A, working from row 1 of chart [K10A, 5C, 10A], K4(6)A, pat across row 19 of chart, then K3(5)A.
Continue in pat as now set until row 38 of first 2 motifs has been completed, then continue with 3rd motif only for another 6 rows.

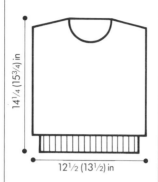

14¼ (15¾) in

12½ (13½) in

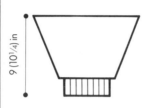

9 (10¼) in

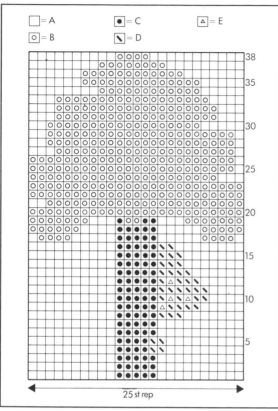

□ = A   ◉ = C   △ = E

◎ = B   ◣ = D

25 st rep

(row numbers shown: 5, 10, 15, 20, 25, 30, 35, 38)

Now place 4th and 5th motifs at the same position in the row as first and second and continue in pat until row 38 of third motif has been completed, then continue with 4th and 5th motifs only for another 6 rows. Continue in this way, placing the 6th motif above the 3rd, then the 7th and 8th above the 4th and 5th, working 6 rows in between, until row 18(32) of the 7th and 8th motifs has been worked.

Shape shoulders
Bind off 14(15) sts at beg of next 4 rows.
Break off yarn and leave remaining 33(37) sts on a holder.

FRONT
Work as for back until front measures 26 rows less than back to shoulders, so ending with a wrong-side row.

Shape neck
Next row: Pat across 36(38) sts, turn and leave remaining sts on a holder.
Dec 1 st at neck edge on the next 3 rows, then on every other row until 28(30) sts remain.
Work straight until front measures same as back to shoulder, ending at armhole edge.

Shape shoulder
Bind off 14(15) sts at beg of next row.
Work 1 row, then bind off.
Return to remaining sts.
With right side facing, slip first 17(21) sts onto a

holder, rejoin yarn and pat to end of row. Complete to match first side of neck, reversing all shaping.

SLEEVES
Using smaller needles and A, cast on 35(41) sts.
Work 2" in rib as for back, ending with rib row 1.
Inc row: Rib 4(7), ✲ M1, rib 3, rep from ✲ to last 4(7) sts, M1, rib to end: 45(51) sts.
Change to larger needles.
Beg with a K row and increasing 1 st each end of 3rd row, work 4 rows st st: 47(53) sts.
Now place motifs as follows:
Next row: K11(14)A, working from chart [K10A, 5C, 10A], then K11(14)A.
Increasing 1 st each end of next and every following 3rd row, continue to work from chart as set until row 22 has been completed: 61(67) sts.
Now place 2nd and 3rd motifs as follows:
Next row: Inc in first st, pat as given for last 13(16) sts of first row of chart, K4A, pat across next 25 sts from row 23 of chart, K4A, pat as given for first 13(16) sts of first row of chart, then inc in last st: 63(69) sts.
Continuing to inc each end of every following 3rd row as before, work motifs from chart as set until row 38 of first motif has been completed, then continue with 2nd and 3rd motifs for another 6 rows: 77(83) sts.
Place 4th motif as follows:
Next row: Pat across first 22(25) sts, K4A, working from chart [K10A, 5C, 10A], K4A, pat across last 22(25) sts.
Continue as set, increasing every 3rd row as before until there are 85(91) sts.
Work straight until row 38 of the 2nd and 3rd motifs has been completed.
2nd size only
Work another 12 rows straight.
Both sizes
Bind off.

NECKBAND
Join right shoulder seam.
With right side facing and using smaller needles and A, pick up and K20 sts down left side of front neck, K across 17(21) sts from front neck holder, pick up and K20 sts up right side of front neck, then K across 33(37) sts from back neck holder: 90(98) sts.
Work 1" in K1, P1 rib. Bind off in rib.

TO FINISH
Press or block, as appropriate for yarn used.
Join left shoulder seam, leaving 3" open at neck edge.
Placing center of top of sleeves at shoulder seam, sew in sleeves.
Join side and sleeve seams. Make 3 button loops on front edge of shoulder opening, then sew on buttons to match.

BREAKFAST TIME

Teddy bear bibs for baby and bear!

MATERIALS

2 oz [50 g] of a cotton fingering yarn, such as Phildar Perlé No 5, in main color A

Small amount of yarn for teddy motif in contrasting color B

Small amount of black for embroidered features

A pair of size 4 double-pointed knitting needles for child's bib

A pair of size 2 double-pointed knitting needles for Teddy's bib

GAUGE

24 sts and 36 rows to 4" measured over seed st worked on larger needles using yarn double

30 sts and 48 rows to 4" measured over seed st worked on smaller needles using yarn single

To save time, take time to check gauge.

NOTES

Instructions given are for Teddy's bib; the instructions for the child's bib are given in parentheses. The Teddy's bib is worked throughout using the yarn single, and the child's bib is worked throughout using the yarn double.

INSTRUCTIONS

TO MAKE

Using smaller (larger) needles and 1(2) strands of A, cast on 23 sts.

Row 1: K twice into first st, [P1, K1] to last 2 sts, P twice into next st, K1: 25 sts.

Row 2: K twice into first st, [K1, P1] to last 2 sts, P twice into next st, K1: 27 sts.

Rep these 2 rows 3 more times: 39 sts.

Work 16 rows straight in seed st.

Now work from chart on page 94 as follows:

Row 1: Seed st 7, K25, seed st 7.

Row 2: Seed st 7, P25, seed st 7.

Row 3: Seed st 7A, K4A, 5B, 7A, 5B, 4A, seed st 7A.

Row 4: Seed st 7A, P3A, 7B, 5A, 7B, 3A, seed st 7A.

Working 7 sts in seed st at each end of the rows, continue in pat from chart, working single motif only, until row 25 has been completed. Using A only, work 6 rows st st.

Work 10 rows seed st across all sts, so ending with a right-side row.

Shape neck

Next row: Seed st 14, bind off 11 sts, seed st to end.

Working on first 14 sts only, dec 1 st at neck edge on next 5 rows: 9 sts.

Work 5 rows seed st.

Shape shoulder

Next row: Bind off 5 sts, K to end.

Next row: P to end: 4 sts.

Now continue in tubular knitting as follows: K1 row.

★ Slide the sts to the other end of the needle, then bringing the yarn across the back of the work and pulling it fairly tightly, K the 4 sts again. ★

Rep from ★ to ★ until piece measures 9(10)".

Bind off. Return to remaining sts.

With right side facing, join yarn to remaining sts and complete to match first side of neck, reversing all shaping and working 1 extra row before shaping shoulder.

TO FINISH

Darn in all ends neatly, and gather tops of ties to close. Press lightly on wrong side.

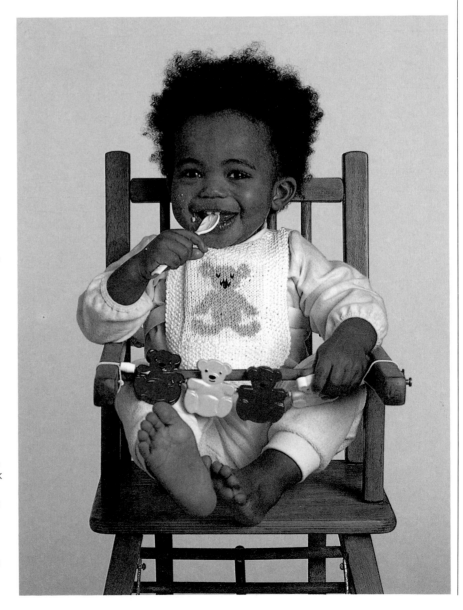

Whether it's porridge on the menu or not, a bib really is a must when you're learning to feed yourself! The bear on this bib is knitted or duplicate-stitched on a plain knit panel surrounded by seed stitch. And there's a smaller version for Teddy, too (see page 97).

INSIDE OUT

A warm hooded jacket with turn-back cuffs and an easy front fastening.

MEASUREMENTS
To fit 16(18,20,22)" chest
Actual measurements 21(23,25,27)"
Length from shoulder 11(12,13,14)"
Sleeve seam 7(8,9,10)"

MATERIALS
13 oz [350 g] of a smooth lightweight yarn, such as Phildar Luxe, in color A
6(6,8,8) oz [150(150,200,200) g] of a lightweight mohair blend, such as Phildar Anouchka, in color B
A pair of size 2 knitting needles
2 stitch holders

GAUGE
29 sts and 40 rows to 4" measured over st st using smooth yarn
29 sts and 36 rows to 4" measured over st st using mohair blend

To save time, take time to check gauge.

INSTRUCTIONS

OUTER JACKET BACK
Using A, cast on 79(85,93,99) sts. Beg with a K row, work in st st until back measures 6(6,6½,7)" from beg, ending with a P row. Place a marker each end of last row to denote beg of armholes.
Continue in st st until back measures 10½(11½,12½, 13½)" from beg, ending with a P row.
Shape back neck
Next row: K20(22,24,26), K2 tog, turn and leave remaining sts on a spare needle.
Dec 1 st at neck edge on every row until 16(18,20,22) sts remain.
Bind off. Return to remaining sts.
With right side facing, slip first 35(37,41,43) sts onto a holder, rejoin yarn, then K2 tog, K to end.
Now complete to match first side of neck, reversing all shaping.

INNER JACKET BACK
Using B, work as for outer jacket back.

OUTER JACKET RIGHT FRONT
Using A, cast on 59(63,69,73) sts. Work in st st until front measures same as back to armholes, ending with a P row.
Place a marker at beg of last row to denote beg of armhole.
Continue in st st until front measures 2" less than

back to shoulder, ending with a P row.
Shape neck
Bind off 24(26,28,30) sts, work until there are 7(7,9,9) sts on needle, then slip these sts onto a safety-pin, work 2 tog, work to end.
Dec 1 st at neck edge on every row until 16(18,20,22) sts remain.
Work straight until front measures same as back to shoulders. Bind off.

INNER JACKET RIGHT FRONT
Using B, work as for outer jacket right front.

OUTER JACKET LEFT FRONT
Work as for outer jacket right front but end with a K row before placing armhole marker or shaping neck.

INNER JACKET LEFT FRONT
Using B, work as for outer jacket right front except end with a K row before placing armhole marker or shaping neck.

SLEEVES
Using A, cast on 73(87,93,101) sts for top of sleeve.
Beg with a K row, work 8(6,14,24) rows in st st.
Dec 1 st each end of next and every following 4th row until 51(59,65,73) sts remain.
Work straight until sleeve measures 7(8,9,10)", ending with a K row.
K1 row to form ridge on right side.
Break off A and join on B.
Continue in st st for 2".
Inc 1 st each end of next and every following 4th row until there are 73(87,93,101) sts.
Work straight until inner sleeve lining measures the same as outer sleeve when sleeve is folded along garter st ridge.
Bind off.

OUTER JACKET HOOD
Join shoulder seams of outer and inner jacket.
With right side of outer jacket facing, slip 7(7,9,9) sts from safety-pin at right front onto a needle, join on A and cast on 8(8,10,10) sts, then K the 7(7,9,9) sts, pick up and K20 sts up right side of front neck, 6 sts down right back neck, decreasing 1 st at center, K across 35(37,41,43) sts from back neck holder, pick up and K6 sts up left side of back neck and 20 sts down left side of front neck, then K across 7(7,9,9) sts from safety-pin at left front neck.
Next row: Cast on 8(8,10,10) sts, P these sts, then P to end: 116(118,130,132) sts.
Continue in st st until hood measures 6¼(6¾,7,8)" from beg, ending with a P row.
Shape crown
Next row: K55(56,62,63), K2 tog, K2, K2 tog tbl, K to end. Work 3 rows straight.

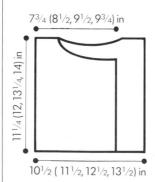

7¾ (8½,9½,9¾) in

11¼ (12,13¼,14) in

10½ (11½,12½,13½) in

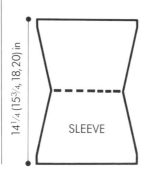

14¼ (15¾,18,20) in

SLEEVE

Next row: K54(55,61,62), K2 tog, K2, K2 tog tbl, K to end.
Work 3 rows straight.
Continue decreasing in this way, working 1 st less each side on every 4th row, until 102(102,112,114) sts remain.
Work 1 row straight.
Now either divide the remaining sts onto 2 needles for grafting together or bind off.

INNER JACKET HOOD
Work as for outer jacket hood.

TO FINISH
Press or block, according to yarn used.
Join top seams on outer and inner hood. Sew in sleeves between markers, then join side and sleeve seams, first on outer and then on inner jacket. Pull sleeve linings into place inside outer jacket sleeves. Join outer jacket edges to lining along fronts and around hood, then finally join jacket to lining all along lower edges.
Make 2 button loops in A on right front edge and 2 button loops in B on left front edge. Sew on buttons to match.

Even though it's knitted in a fine yarn, this hooded jacket will keep little ones warm as toast. It is reversible – and thus double thickness – and makes a smart outfit with the Teddy Overalls on page 106.

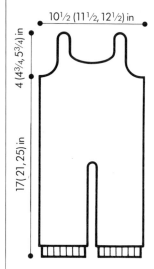

10½ (11½, 12½) in

4 (4¾, 5¾) in

17 (21, 25) in

WALKABOUT

Overalls with a sitting bear motif on the front.

MEASUREMENTS

To fit 16–18(20,22)" chest
Actual measurements 21(23,25)"
Length from armhole to ankle 17(21,25)"

MATERIALS

13 oz [350 g] of a smooth lightweight yarn, such as
Pingouin Pingofine
Small amount of contrasting yarn for motif
A pair of size 2 knitting needles and one size 2
circular needle 16" long
2 stitch holders
2 buttons

GAUGE

29 sts and 40 rows to 4" measured over st st

To save time, take time to check gauge.

INSTRUCTIONS

RIGHT LEG

★ Using the pair of needles cast on
39(43,47) sts.
Rib row 1: K2, ✻ P1, K1, rep from ✻ to last st, K1.
Rib row 2: K1, ✻ P1, K1, rep from ✻ to end.
Rep these 2 rows for 2(2,3)", ending with rib row 2.
Make hem as follows:
Next row: K1, then folding ribbing in half to wrong
side, pick up first loop from cast-on edge and place
on left-hand needle, then K the loop, K1, ✻ pick up
next loop from cast-on edge and place on left-hand
needle, K the loop, then K1, rep from ✻ to end:
78(86,94) sts. P1 row.
Beg with a K row, work in st st until leg measures
9(11,13)" from lower edge of hem, ending with a
P row. ★
Break off yarn and leave sts on a spare needle.

LEFT LEG

Work as for right leg from ★ to ★ .
Change to circular needle.
First round: K39(43,47), place a loop of contrasting
yarn on needle to denote left side edge, K to last st
of left leg, K tog last st of left leg with first st of right
leg, K38(42,46), place a loop of contrasting yarn on
needle to denote right side edge, K to last st of right
leg, place a contrasting loop of yarn on needle to
denote center back, then K tog last st of right leg with
first st of left leg: 154(170,186) sts.
Slipping markers on every row, continue in
st st until work measures 7½(9½,11½)" from crotch,
ending at center back marker.

Break off yarn and slip first 39(43,47) sts up to
marker onto a holder.

Divide for back and front

Using the pair of needles work across the first
77(85,93) sts for front as follows:
Next row: K1, ✻ P1, K1, rep from ✻ to next marker,
turn and leave remaining sts on a holder.
Seed st row: K1, ✻ P1, K1, rep from ✻ to end.
Rep this row 4 more times.

Shape armholes

Bind off 6(6,8) sts at beg of next 2 rows: 65(73,77) sts.
Keeping pat correct, dec 1 st each end of every row
until 49(53,57) sts remain.
Work straight until bib measures 1½(2,2)" from beg
of armhole shaping, ending with a right-side row.

Shape neck

Next row: Seed st 19, bind off 11(15,19), seed st to
end.
Working on first set off sts only, dec 1 st at neck edge
on next 10 rows: 9 sts.
Work straight until strap measures 1½(2,3)" from
beg of neck shaping, ending with a wrong-side row.

Place buttonhole

Row 1: [K1,P1] twice, wind yarn twice around
needle, skpo, K1, P1, K1.
Row 2: [K1,P1] twice, K once into large loop, [P1,
K1] twice. Work 4 rows seed st.
★★ Dec 1 st each end of next row; work one row
straight; dec one st each end of next row: 5 sts. Bind
off. ★★
Return to remaining sts.
With right side facing, rejoin yarn and complete 2nd
side of neck to match first, reversing all shaping.
Now return to remaining sts for back.
With right side facing, rejoin yarn and work in seed st
across all 77(85,93) sts.
Work 5 more rows seed st.
Now complete as for front bib, except work in seed
st until straps are 3(4,6)" long, then omitting
buttonholes, shape top as from ★★ to ★★ .

POCKET (optional)

Using pair of needles cast on 35 sts.
Work 6 rows seed st.
Next row (right side): Seed st 5, K25, seed st 5.
Next row: Seed st 5, P25, seed st 5.
Rep these 2 rows 14 more times, then the first row
again.
Work 6 rows seed st over all sts, so ending with a
right-side row. Bind off knitwise.

TO FINISH

Press or block, as appropriate for yarn used.
Join inside leg seams and short underarm seam.
Duplicate stitch Teddy motif from page 94 either on
pocket or on front of overalls as shown. Sew on
pocket if used. Sew on buttons and finish
buttonholes.

The pocket on the chest of these overalls is
popular with toddlers, but for smaller babies it can be omitted
and the bear motif placed directly on the front of the overalls.

CROSS COUNTRY

A long-sleeved pullover with a cross-over roll neck.

MEASUREMENTS
To fit 18(20,22)" chest
Actual measurements 22(24,26)"
Length from shoulder 11(12,13)"
Sleeve seam 7(8,9)"

MATERIALS
6(8,8) oz [150(200,200) g] of a smooth medium-weight yarn, such as Phildar Pronostic, in main color A
2 oz [50 g] of same in each of contrasting colors B, C and D
A pair each of size 2 and size 4 knitting needles and one size 2 circular needle, any length
Stitch holder

GAUGE
24 sts and 52 rows to 4" measured over pattern worked on larger needles

To save time, take time to check gauge.

INSTRUCTIONS

BACK
★ Using pair of smaller needles and A, cast on 65(71,77) sts.
Rib row 1: K1, ★ P1, K1, rep from ★ to end.
Rib row 2: K2, ★ P1, K1, rep from ★ to last st, K1.
Rep these 2 rows for 1½", ending with rib row 1.
Increasing 1 st each end, K1 row: 67(73,79) sts.
Change to larger needles. Joining on and cutting off colors as required, proceed in pat as follows:
Row 1: With B, K1, ★ sl 1 pw, K1, rep from ★ to end.
Row 2: With B, K1, ★ yfwd, sl 1 pw, ybk, K1, rep from ★ to end.
Rows 3 and 4: With A, K to end.
Row 5: With C, K2, ★ sl 1 pw, K1, rep from ★ to last st, K1.
Row 6: With C, K2, ★ yfwd, sl 1 pw, ybk, K1, rep from ★ to last st, K1.
Rows 7 and 8: With A, K to end.
Rows 9 and 10: With D, as rows 1 and 2.
Rows 11 and 12: With A, K to end.
Rows 13 and 14: With B, as rows 5 and 6.
Rows 15 and 16: With A, K to end.
Rows 17 and 18: With C, as rows 1 and 2.
Rows 19 and 20: With A, K to end.
Rows 21 and 22: With D, as rows 5 and 6.
Rows 23 and 24: With A, K to end.
These 24 rows form the pat.
Continue in pat until back measures 6(7,7½)" from beg, ending with a wrong-side row in A.

Place a marker each end of last row to denote beg of armholes. ★
Continue in pat until back measures 11(12,13)" from beg, ending with a right-side row in A.
Next row: Bind off 18(21,24), K to end.
Next row: Bind off 18(21,24), then slip remaining 31 sts onto a holder.

FRONT
Work as for back from ★ to ★.
Continue in pat until front measures 7(8,9)" from beg, ending with a right-side row in A.
Divide for neck
Next row: K18(21,24), bind off next 31 sts, K to end.
Work straight on first set of sts until front measures same as back to shoulders, ending with a wrong-side row in A. Bind off. Return to remaining sts.
With right side facing, rejoin yarn and pat to end.
Now complete to match first side of neck.

SLEEVES
Using smaller needles and A, cast on 37(39,41) sts.
Work 1½" in rib as for back, ending with rib row 1.
Increasing 1 st each end, K1 row: 39(41,43) sts.
Change to larger needles.
Work in pat as for back, increasing and working into pat 1 st each end of 5th and every following 4th(4th,6th) row until there are 63(63,69) sts.
Work straight until sleeve measures 7(8,9)" from beg, ending with a wrong-side row in A.
Using A, bind off.

COLLAR
Join shoulder seams.
With right side facing, using circular needle and A, pick up and K38 sts up right side of front neck, K across 31 sts from back neck holder, then pick up and K38 sts down left side of front neck: 107 sts.
K1 row.
Beg with rib row 1 and working backward and forward in rows, work in rib as for back for 5", ending with rib row 2.
Bind off knitwise.

TO FINISH
Press or block, as appropriate for yarn used.
Sew in sleeves between markers, then join side and sleeve seams. Sew down row ends of collar, lapping left over right for a boy or right over left for a girl.

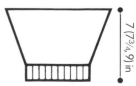 Perfect for a crisp fall day, this warm sweater is easy to get in and out of because of the generous cross-over neck opening. The dotted effect is achieved by slip-stitching the main color every two rows.

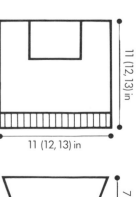

CHRISTMAS STOCKING

Just like a real Christmas stocking, this chapter is bursting with good things! The designs have been created in bright, festive colors and in warm wool yarns to keep out the cold. The patterns include a classic party dress, a snowflake motif Fair Isle sweater, and a cozy hat and scarf set. And there are motifs for Christmas trees, snowmen, reindeer, and a special Christmas star.

NOËL NOËL

A classic lacy dress, with short sleeves and a full skirt.

MEASUREMENTS
To fit 20(22)" chest
Actual measurements 21(23)"
Length from shoulder 19¼"
Sleeve seam ¾"

MATERIALS
9(11)oz (250[300]g) of a medium-weight brushed acrylic-blend yarn such as Patons Promise D.K.
A pair of size 5 knitting needles
3 buttons
1 yard of wide ribbon for sash

GAUGE
22 sts and 30 rows to 4" measured over pat.

To save time, take time to check gauge.

INSTRUCTIONS

FRONT
★ Cast on 113(119) sts. Work in pat as follows:
Row 1: K2(5), ★ yo, K2 tog, K10, rep from ★ to last 3(6) sts, yo, K2 tog, K1(4).
Row 2 and every other row: P to end.
Row 3: K3(6), ★ yo, K2 tog, K7, skpo, yo, K1, rep from ★ to last 2(5) sts, K2(5).

Party dresses have to be special, and these will certainly not disappoint; little girls love the lacy texture and the full skirts. The effect is completed with satin petticoats, ribbon sashes, and ballet slippers.

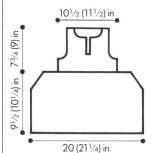

10½ (11½) in

7¾ (9) in

9½ (10¼) in

20 (21¼) in

¾ in

11½ (12½) in

Row 5: K3(6), ✷ K1, yo, K2 tog, K5, skpo, yo, K2, rep from ✷ to last 2(5) sts, K2(5).
Row 7: As row 3.
Row 9: As row 3.
Row 11: K to end.
Row 13: K to end.
Row 15: K8(11), ✷ yo, K2 tog, K10, rep from ✷ to last 9(12) sts, yo, K2 tog, K7(10).
Row 17: K6(9), ✷ skpo, yo, K1, yo, K2 tog, K7, rep from ✷ to last 11(14) sts, skpo, yo, K1, yo, K2 tog, K6(9).
Row 19: K5(8), ✷ skpo, yo, K3, yo, K2 tog, K5;
for 1st size only rep from ✷ to end;
for 2nd size only rep from ✷ to last 3 sts, K3.
Row 21: As row 17.
Row 23: As row 17.
Row 25: K to end.
Row 27: K to end.
Row 28: P to end.
These 28 rows form the pat.
Continue in pat until work measures 8(8¾)" from beg, ending with a 4th or 18th row of pat.
Side shaping
Keeping pat correct, dec 1 st each end of next 12 rows: 89(95) sts.
Shape waist
Dec row: for 2nd size only K3;
for both sizes ✷ K2 tog, K1, rep from ✷ to last 2 sts;
for 1st size only K2 tog;
for 2nd size only K2: 59(65) sts.
P1 row.
Place a marker at each end of last row to denote waist.
Working in pat as for 2nd(1st) size, continue without shaping until work measures 2½(3)" from markers, ending with a wrong-side row.
Shape armholes
Bind off 4 sts at beg of next 2 rows.
Keeping pat correct, dec 1 st each end of next 4 rows: 43(49) sts. ★
Divide for front neck opening
Next row: Pat 22(25), turn and leave remaining sts on a spare needle.
Work straight in pat until work measures 5½(6½)" from markers, ending with a right-side row.
Shape neck
Bind off 11 sts at beg of nex row. Dec 1 st at neck edge on next 3 rows: 8(11) sts.
Work straight until work measures 8(9)" from markers, ending with a wrong-side row.
Bind off.
Return to remaining sts.
With right side facing, join on yarn and pat to end of row: 21(24) sts.
Work straight in pat until work measures 5½(6½)" from markers, ending with a wrong-side row.
Shape neck
Bind off 10 sts at beg of next row.

Dec 1 st at neck edge on next 3 rows: 8(11) sts.
Now complete to match first side of neck.

BACK
Work as for front from ★ to ★ .
Work straight until work measures 8(9)" from markers, ending with a wrong-side row.
Bind off 8(11) sts at beg of next 2 rows.
Bind off remaining 27 sts.

SLEEVES
Cast on 65(71) sts.
Work in pat as for back for ¾".
Shape top
Bind off 4 sts at beg of next 2 rows.
Keeping pat correct, dec 1 st each end of next 4 rows, then each end of every other row until 41(47) sts remain.
Now dec 1 st each end of every row until 13(17) sts remain.
Bind off.

PICOT HEM
With right side facing, pick up and K113(119) sts along lower edge of back.
P 1 row.
Picot edge: Bind off 2 sts, ✷ slip st from right-hand needle back onto left-hand needle, cast on 2 sts, then bind off 4 sts, rep from ✷ to end.
Rep along lower edge of front.

SLEEVE EDGINGS
Work as for picot hem, picking up 65(71) sts along lower edge of sleeve.

NECKBAND
Join shoulder seams.
With right side facing, pick up and K83 sts evenly around neck edge.
Complete as for picot hem.

TO FINISH
Block the work. Sew in sleeves, easing in fullness to fit. Join side and sleeve seams. Make 3 button loops down right front edge. Sew on buttons opposite loops, on left front. Make 2 large loops on waist at side seam, then thread sash through.

"Christmas is coming
  The Goose is getting fat,
Please put a penny
  In the old man's hat
If you haven't got a penny
  A hu'penny will do,
If you haven't got a ha'penny,
  Then God bless you."

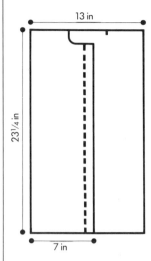

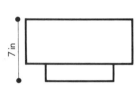

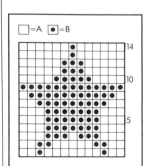

STAR BRIGHT

A warm, hooded baby's sleeping bag with a sparkling Christmas star motif.

MEASUREMENTS

To fit 16–18" chest
Actual measurement 26"
Length 23"
Sleeve seam 7"

MATERIALS

13 oz (350 g) of a smooth medium-weight yarn, such as Rowan Lightweight D.K.
Small amount of a lightweight glitter yarn, such as Twilleys Goldfingering, for embroidered star motif
8 buttons
A pair each of size 3 and size 5 knitting needles
Stitch holder

GAUGE

24 sts and 48 rows to 4" measured over pattern using larger needles

To save time, take time to check gauge.

INSTRUCTIONS

BACK

Using smaller needles cast on 81 sts.
K 3 rows.
Change to larger needles.
Work in pat as follows:
Row 1: K2, ✲ sl 1, K1, rep from ✲ to last st, K1.
Row 2: K2, ✲ yfwd, sl 1, ybk, K1, rep from ✲ to last st, K1.
Rows 3 and 4: K to end.
These 4 rows form the pat.
Continue in pat until back measures 23" from beg, or desired length – ending with row 2 of pat.
Bind off 27 sts at beg of next 2 rows.
Break off yarn and leave remaining 27 sts on a holder.

LEFT FRONT

Using smaller needles cast on 44 sts.
K 3 rows.
Change to larger needles.
Work in pat with seed st border as follows:
Row 1: K2, ✲ sl 1, K1, rep from ✲ to last 6 sts, [P1, K1] twice, P1, sl 1.
Row 2: [K1, P1] 3 times, K1, ✲ yfwd, sl 1, ybk, K1, rep from ✲ to last st, K1.
Row 3: K to last 6 sts, [P1, K1] twice, P1, sl 1.
Row 4: [K1, P1] 3 times, K to end.
These 4 rows form the pat with seed st border.
Continue in pat until front measures 18" from beg, ending with row 2 of pat.

Place st st square
Next row (right side): K to last 6 sts, seed st 6.
Next row: Seed st 6, K7, P17, K14.
Next row: Pat 14, K17, pat 7, seed st 6.
Next row: Seed st 6, pat 7, P17, pat 14.
Rep these last 4 rows three more times, then the first 2 rows again.
Continue in pat with seed st border across all sts until front measures 20 rows less than back to shoulders.
Shape neck
Next row: Pat to last 6 sts, seed st 6.
Next row: Bind off 6 sts purlwise, pat to end: 38 sts.
Next row: Pat to last 6 sts, K2 tog, K1, turn and leave remaining 3 sts on a safety-pin.
Keeping pat correct, dec 1 st at neck edge on every row until 27 sts remain.
Work straight until front measures same as back to shoulder.
Bind off.
Mark positions on seed st border for 8 buttons, the first one 3" from lower edge, the top one ¾" from neck edge and the others spaced evenly in between.

RIGHT FRONT

Using smaller needles cast on 44 sts.
K 3 rows.
Change to larger needles.
Work in pat with seed st border as follows:
Row 1 (right side): [K1, P1] 3 times, ✲ K1, sl 1, rep from ✲ to last 2 sts, K2.
Row 2: K2, ✲ yfwd, sl 1, ybk, K1, rep from ✲ to last 6 sts, [P1, K1] twice, P1, sl 1.
Row 3: [K1, P1] 3 times, K to end.
Row 4: K to last 6 sts, [P1, K1] twice, P1, sl 1.
These 4 rows form pat with seed st border.
Continue in pat until front measures 20 rows less than back to shoulders and AT THE SAME TIME work buttonholes opposite markers as fallows:
Buttonhole row (right side): K1, P1, K1, yo, skpo, P1, pat to end.
Shape neck
Next row: Bind off 6 sts, pat to end.
Next row: Pat to last 3 sts, turn and leave remaining 3 sts on a safety-pin.
Now complete to match left front, reversing all shaping.

SLEEVES

Using smaller needles cast on 37 sts.
Rib row 1: K2, ✲ P1, K1, rep from ✲ to last st, K1.
Rib row 2: K1, ✲ P1, K1, rep from ✲ to end.
Rep these 2 rows for 2", ending with rib row 2.
Change to larger needles.
Inc row: K into front and back of every st: 74 sts.
Next row: K to end, inc in last st: 75 sts.
Now work in pat as for back until sleeve measures 7" from beg, ending with row 4 of pat. Bind off.

NECKBAND AND HOOD

Join shoulder seams.

With right side facing and using smaller needles, join on yarn at right front neck edge and K3 sts from safety-pin, pick up and K19 sts up right side of neck, K across 27 sts from back neck holder, pick up and K19 sts down left front neck, then K3 sts from safety-pin: 71 sts.

Beg with a rib row 2, work 3 rows rib.

Change to larger needles.

Inc row: Rib 8, [inc in next st, rib 7] 7 times, inc in next st, rib to end: 79 sts.

Next row: K to end.

Now work in pat as for back until hood measures 5" from beg, ending with row 2 of pat.

Shape crown

Row 1: K37, K2 tog, K1, K2 tog tbl, K to end.

Pat 3 rows.

Row 5: K36, K2 tog, K1, K2 tog tbl, K to end.

Pat 3 rows.

Continue decreasing each side of center st on next and every following 4th row until 67 sts remain.

Pat 1 row, so ending with a wrong-side row.

Bind off purlwise.

TO FINISH

Join seam at top of hood.

Border: With right side facing and using smaller needles, pick up and K81 sts evenly around edge of hood.

K 1 row.

Change to larger needles and bind off purlwise. Sew in sleeves, then join side and sleeve seams. Finish buttonholes and sew on buttons. Using 2 strands of glitter yarn duplicate stitch star motif on st st square at top of left front. Join lower edge of sleeping bag if desired, lapping buttonhole border over button border.

 This roomy sleeping bag for a baby is knitted in a medium-weight yarn, which makes it warm without being bulky. When he or she is old enough to stand, you can undo the lower seam and *violà!* you will have a hooded bathrobe.

GO FOR GOLD

A smart V-neck slipover with matching bow tie.

MEASUREMENTS
Child's slipover
To fit 18(20,22)" chest
Actual measurements 21½(23,24½)"
Length from shoulder 11(12,13)"
Teddy's slipover
To fit 15" chest

MATERIALS
Child's slipover
2(2,4) oz (50[50,100] g) of a smooth lightweight yarn, such as Pingouin Pingofine, in main color A
Teddy's slipover
2oz (50g) of same in main color A
Both slipovers
1oz (25g) of a lightweight glitter yarn, such as Twilleys Goldfingering, in contrasting color B
A pair each of size 0 and size 2 knitting needles
Stitch holder
Bow Tie
Small amount of contrasting color B
A pair of size 1 knitting needles
Size C crochet hook

GAUGE
32 sts and 40 rows to 4" measured over st st worked on largest needles

To save time, take time to check gauge.

INSTRUCTIONS FOR CHILD'S SLIPOVER

FRONT
★ Using smallest needles and A, cast on 85(91,97) sts.
Rib row 1: K2, ★ P1, K1, rep from ★ to last st, K1.
Rib row 2: K1, ★ P1, K1, rep from ★ to end.
Rep these 2 rows for 1(1½,1½)", ending rib row 2. Change to largest needles.
Inc row: K21(24,27), ★ inc in next st, K20, rep from ★ once more, inc in next st, K21(24,27): 88(94,100) sts.
P 1 row. ★
Work in Square pat as follows:
Row 1: K1B, ★ 2A, 4B, rep from ★ to last 3 sts, K2A, 1B.
Row 2: P1B, ★ 2A, 4B, rep from ★ to last 3 sts, P2A, 1B.
Rows 3 and 4: As rows 1 and 2.
Row 5: K with A.
Row 6: P with A.
These 6 rows form the pat.
Continue in pat until front measures 5½(6½,7½)" from beg, ending with a wrong-side row.
Shape armholes
Bind off 4 sts at beg of next 2 rows: 80(86,92) sts.

Divide for neck
Keeping pat correct, K2 tog, pat next 38(41,44) sts, turn and leave remaining sts on a spare needle.
Dec 1 st at armhole edge on the next 8 rows, then on every other row 3 times, AT THE SAME TIME dec 1 st at neck edge on the 2nd and every other row until 8(11,14) sts remain.
Work straight until front measures 11(12,13)" from beg, ending with row 6 of pat. Bind off.
Return to remaining sts.
With right side facing, join on yarns and pat to last 2 sts, K2 tog: 39(42,45) sts.
Now complete to match first side of neck, reversing all shaping.

BACK
Work as for front from ★ to ★.
Using A only, continue in st st until back measures same as front to armholes, ending with a P row.

Shape armholes
Bind off 4 sts at beg of next 2 rows.
Dec 1 st each end of next 9 rows: 62(68,74) sts.
Now dec 1 st each end of every other row 3 times: 56(62,68) sts.
Work straight until back measures 4 rows less than front, ending with a P row.
Shape neck
Next row: K10(13,16), K2 tog, turn and leave remaining sts on a spare needle.
Dec 1 st at neck edge on next 3 rows.
Bind off. Return to remaining sts.
With right side facing, slip first 32 sts onto a holder, join on yarn, K2 tog, K to end.
Now complete to match first side of neck, reversing all shaping.

NECKBAND
Join left shoulder seam.
With right side facing and using smallest needles and A, pick up and K53 sts down right side of front neck.
Work 7 rows in rib as for back.
Bind off.
With right side facing and using smallest needles and A, pick up and K4 sts down right side of back neck, K across 32 sts on back neck holder, pick up and K4 sts up left side of back neck and 53 sts down left side of front neck: 93 sts.
Work 7 rows in rib as for back.
Bind off.

ARMHOLE BORDERS
Join right shoulder and neckband seam.
With right side facing and using smallest needles and A, pick up and K103 sts evenly around armhole edge.
Complete as for neckband.

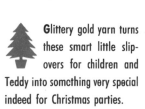
Glittery gold yarn turns these smart little slip-overs for children and Teddy into something very special indeed for Christmas parties.

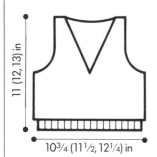

11 (12, 13) in

10¾ (11½, 12¼) in

TO FINISH
Press or block, as appropriate for yard used. Crossing left over right for a boy or right over left for a girl, sew front neckband edges in place. Join side and armhole border seams.

INSTRUCTIONS FOR TEDDY'S SLIPOVER

FRONT
★★ Using smallest needles and A, cast on 69 sts. Work in rib as for front of child's slipover for 8 rows. Change to largest needles.
Work 2 rows st st, increasing 1 st at beg of first row: 70 sts. ★★
Now work in pat as for front of child's slipover until front measures 3½" from beg, ending with a wrong-side row.
Place a marker at each end of last row to denote beg of armholes.
Divide for neck
Next row: Pat 33, K2 tog, turn and leave remaining sts on a spare needle.
Keeping pat correct, dec 1 st at neck edge on every other row until 16 sts remain.
Work straight until front measures 7½" from beg, ending with row 6 of pat.
Bind off.
Return to remaining sts.
With right side facing, join on yarns, K2 tog, pat to end of row.
Now complete to match first side of neck, reversing all shaping.

BACK
Work as for front from ★★ to ★★.
Using A only, work in st st until back measures same as front to armhole markers, ending with a P row.
Place a marker at each end of last row.
Continue in st st until back measures 4 rows less than front, ending with a P row.
Shape neck
Next row: K18, K2 tog, turn and leave remaining sts on a spare needle.
Dec 1 st at neck edge on next 3 rows.
Bind off.
Return to remaining sts.
With right side facing, slip first 30 sts onto a holder, join on yarn, K2 tog, K to end.
Now complete to match first side of neck, reversing all shaping.

NECKBAND
Join left shoulder seam.
With right side facing and using smallest needles and A, pick up and K41 sts down right side of front neck.
Work 5 rows in rib as for back of child's slipover. Now bind off.

With right side facing and using smallest needles and A, pick up and K4 sts down right side of back neck, K across 30 sts on back neck holder, pick up and K4 sts up left side of back neck and 41 sts down left side of front neck: 79 sts.
Work 5 rows in rib as before. Bind off.

ARMHOLE BORDERS
Join right shoulder and neckband seam.
With right side facing and using smallest needles and A, pick up and K77 sts evenly between markers. Complete as for neckband.

TO FINISH
Press or block, as appropriate for yarn used. Crossing left over right, sew front neckband edges in place. Join side and armhole border seams.

INSTRUCTIONS FOR BOW TIE

NOTE
For the child's bow tie, use the gold yarn double. For Teddy's bow tie, use the gold yarn single.

TO MAKE
Using medium-size knitting needles and B, and using the yarn double or single as appropriate, cast on 1 st.
Row 1: K into front and back of st: 2 sts.
Row 2: K into front and back of first st, K1: 3 sts.
Row 3: K into front and back of first st, P1, K into front and back of last st: 5sts.
Row 4: Inc in first st, K1, P1, K1, inc in last st: 7 sts.
Row 5: K1, [P1, K1] to end.
This last row forms the seed st pat; continue in seed st until work measures 3" from beg.
Shape center of bow
Keeping seed st pat correct, dec 1 st each end of next 2 rows: 3 sts.
Now inc 1 st each end of next 2 rows: 7 sts. Continue in seed st until work measures 6" from beg.
Shape end
Keeping pat correct, dec 1 st each end of next 2 rows, then 1 st at beg of following 2 rows: 1 st. Break yarn and fasten off.

CENTER BAND
Cast on 3 sts.
Seed st row: K1, P1, K1.
Rep this row until band measures 2" from beg. Bind off.

TO FINISH
Using crochet hook, crochet a chain approximately 24" long. Fold bow by placing cast-on and bound-off points at center back and sew in place. Fold band over center of bow and sew at back. Knot crocheted chain over back of band and attach to back of bow with small stitches.

CHRISTMAS TREES

A round-necked, long-sleeved, fuzzy Christmas cardigan decorated all over with bright green fir trees and tiny pearl beads.

MEASUREMENTS

To fit 20(22,24)" chest
Actual measurements 21(24,26)"
Length from shoulder 12½(14,15)"
Sleeve seam 8(9½,10½)"

MATERIALS

4(6,8)oz (100[150,200]g) of a medium-weight mohair, such as Berger Du Nord Kid Mohair, in A. Small amount of Green mohair; 6 pearl buttons A pair each of size 7 and size 9 knitting needles Small pearl beads for decoration; stitch holder

GAUGE

17 sts and 20 rows to 4" measured over st st worked on larger needles

To save time, take time to check gauge.

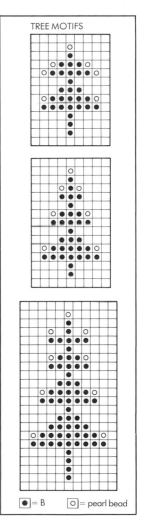

TREE MOTIFS

● = B   ○ = pearl bead

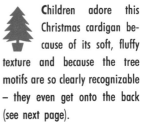

Children adore this Christmas cardigan because of its soft, fluffy texture and because the tree motifs are so clearly recognizable – they even get onto the back (see next page).

The Christmas tree cardigan is seen here from behind; the tree motifs can be placed anywhere you like.

INSTRUCTIONS

BACK
Using smaller needles cast on 44(50,56) sts.
Twisted rib row: ✷ K1 tbl, P1, rep from ✷ to end.
Rep this row 9 more times. Change to larger needles.
Beg with a K row, work in st st until back measures 12½(14,15)" from beg, ending with a P row.
Bind off 14(16,18) sts at beg of next 2 rows.
Break off yarn and leave remaining 16(18,20) sts on a holder.

RIGHT FRONT
Using smaller needles cast on 29(32,35) sts.
Work 4 rows in twisted rib as for back.
Next row: Rib 2, yo, K2 tog, rib to end.
Work 5 more rows in twisted rib.
Next row: Rib 7 and slip these 7 sts onto a safety-pin, change to larger needles, then K to end: 22(25,28) sts.
Beg with a P row, continue in st st until front measures 10 rows less than back to shoulders, ending with a P row.
Shape neck
Row 1 (right side): Bind off 3(4,5) sts, work to end.
Row 2: Work to end.
Row 3: Work 2 tog, work to end.
Row 4: Work to last 2 sts, work 2 tog.
Rows 5 and 6: As rows 3 and 4.
Row 7: As row 3.
Row 8: Work to end: 14(16,18) sts.
Work 2 rows straight. Bind off.

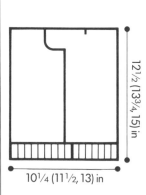
12½ (13¾, 15) in
10¼ (11½, 13) in

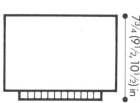
7¾ (9½, 10½) in

LEFT FRONT
Using smaller needles cast on 29(32,35) sts.
Work 10 rows twisted rib as for back.
Next row: K to last 7 sts, turn and leave remaining sts on a safety-pin: 22(25,28) sts.
Now complete to match right front, reversing all shaping.

SLEEVES
Using smaller needles cast on 26(26,28) sts.
Work 7 rows twisted rib.
Inc row: Rib 3(3,2), ✷ K into front and back of next st, rep from ✷ to last 3(3,2) sts, rib to end: 46(46,52) sts.
Change to larger needles.
Beg with K row, work in st st until sleeve measures 7½(9,10¼)" from beg, ending with a P row.
K 5 rows.
Bind off.

NECKBAND
Join shoulder seams.
With right side facing and using smaller needles, join on yarn and pick up and K10 sts up right side of front neck, K16(18,20) sts from back neck holder, then pick up and K10 sts down left side of front neck: 36(38,40) sts.
Work 12 rows in twisted rib.
Bind off loosely in rib.
Fold neckband in half to wrong side and slipstitch in place.

BUTTON BORDER
With right side of left front facing, slip the 7 sts from safety-pin onto a smaller needle, join on yarn, then P1, [K1 tbl, P1] 3 times.
Continue in twisted rib until border, slightly stretched, fits up left front to top of neckband.
Bind off.
Sew on the border, then mark the positions for the 6 buttons, the first one ⅝" from lower edge, the top one ⅝" from bound-off edge and the others spaced evenly in between.

BUTTONHOLE BORDER
With wrong side of right front facing, slip the 7 sts from safety-pin onto a smaller needle, join on yarn, then P1, [K1 tbl, P1] 3 times.
Continue in twisted rib to match button border, working buttonholes opposite markers as follows:
Buttonhole row (right side): Rib 2, yo, K2 tog, rib 3.

TO FINISH
Using green mohair, duplicate stitch tree motifs as desired. Sew on beads to decorate if desired. Fold sleeves in half lengthwise, then placing folds at shoulder seams, sew in place. Join side and sleeve seams.
Sew on buttonhole border. Sew on buttons.

CHRISTMAS WRAPPING

Matching hat, scarf, mittens, and ankle-warmers.

MEASUREMENTS

Hat To fit head up to 20" in circumference
Scarf Length approximately 45"

MATERIALS

11 oz (300g) of a smooth lightweight yarn, such as
Pingouin Pingofine, in main color A
Small amount of White angora (color B)
Small amount of Black smooth yarn (color C)
Small amount of Orange for embroidery
A pair each of size 1, size 2 and size 3 knitting
needles

GAUGE

32 sts and 40 rows to 4" measured over st st worked
on largest needles

To save time, take time to check gauge.

INSTRUCTIONS FOR HAT

Using smallest needles and A, cast on 146 sts.
Work in g st for 1½", ending with a right side row.
Now continue in rib as follows:
Rib row 1 (right side): K2, ✢ P2, K2, rep from ✢ to end.
Rib row 2: K1, P1, ✢ K2, P2, rep from ✢ to last 4 sts,
K2, P1, K1.
Rep these 2 rows for 1¼", ending with rib row 2 and
inc 1 st at end of last row: 147 sts.
Change to largest needles. Beg with a K row, work
in st st for 1", ending with a P row.

 This smart set of mit-
tens, hat, scarf, and
ankle-warmers (see fol-
lowing page) would make a
marvelous Christmas present.
The Baby's mitts (not shown)
are knitted without a thumb to
make them as easy as possible to
put on.

Joining on colors as required work in pat from chart for snowmen as follows:
Row 1: K4A, [7B, 5A] 11 times, 7B, 4A.
Row 2: P3A, [9B, 3A] 12 times.
Continue in pat from chart until row 22 has been completed.
Using A only, continue in st st until hat measures 6" from top of ribbing, ending with a P row.
Shape crown
Row 1: * K2 tog, rep from * to last st, K1: 74 sts.
K5 rows.
Row 7: * K2 tog, rep from * to end: 37 sts. K 5 rows.
Row 13: * K2 tog, rep from * to last st, K1: 19 sts.
K 2 rows.
Break off yarn leaving a long length, thread through sts, draw up tightly and secure.

TO FINISH
Using black, duplicate stitch buttons and eyes on snowmen. Using orange, work a French knot for the nose of each snowman. Join back seam.

INSTRUCTIONS FOR SCARF
Using smallest needles and A, cast on 75 sts.
K 8 rows.
Change to largest needles.
Beg with a K row, work 1½" in st st, ending with a P row.
Joining on colors as required work in pat from chart for snowmen as follows:
Row 1: K5B, [5A, 7B] 5 times, 5A, 5B.
Row 2: P6B, [3A, 9B] 5 times, 3A, 6B.
Continue in pat from chart until row 22 has been completed.
Using A only, continue in st st until scarf measures 41" from beg, ending with a P row.

Now turning chart upside down, work in pat for snowmen as follows:
Row 1: K4C, [7A, 5C] 5 times, 7A, 4C.
Row 2: P5C, [5A, 7C] 5 times, 5A, 5C.
Continue in pat in this way until all 22 rows of chart have been completed.
Working in A only and beg with a K row, work 1½" in st st, ending with a P row.
Change to smallest needles. K 8 rows. Bind off.

TO FINISH
Press or block, as appropriate for yarn used.
Embroider snowmen as for hat. Join center back seam of scarf, taking care to match up the two halves of snowmen at each end. Join lower edges.

INSTRUCTIONS FOR ANKLE-WARMERS
Using medium-size needles and A, cast on 62 sts.
Work in rib as for hat for 2", ending with rib row 2 and inc 1 st at end of last row: 63 sts.
Change to largest needles.
Beg with a K row, work 1¼" in st st, ending with a P row.
Joining on colors as required, work in pat from chart for snowmen as follows:
Row 1: K4A, [7B, 5A] 4 times, 7B, 4A.
Row 2: P3A, [9B, 3A] 5 times.
Continue in pat from chart until row 22 has been completed.
Using A only and beg with a K row, work 1½" st st, ending with a P row and dec 1 st at end of last row: 62 sts.
Change to medium-size needles.
Rep the 2 rib rows for 1¼", ending with rib row 2.
Work 1½" in g st.
Bind off.

TO FINISH
Press or block, as appropriate for yarn used.
Embroider snowmen as for hat. Join seam.

INSTRUCTIONS FOR MITTENS

RIGHT MITTEN
★ Using smallest needles and A, cast on 46 sts.
K 17 rows.
Work in rib as follows:
Rib row 1: K2, * P2, K2, rep from * to end.
Rib row 2: K1, P1, K2, * P2, K2, rep from * to last 2 sts, P1, K1.
Rep these 2 rows 4 more times.
Change to largest needles.
Inc row: K15, * M1, K15, rep from * to last st, K1: 48 sts. ★
Beg with a P row, work 7 rows st st.
Shape thumb gusset
Row 1: K25, M1, K1, M1, K22.
Row 2: P to end.

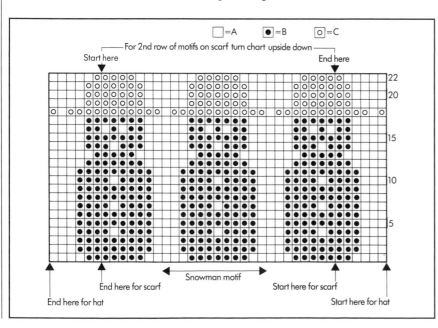

=A   ●=B   ○=C

For 2nd row of motifs on scarf turn chart upside down
Start here   End here
22
20
15
10
5
End here for scarf   Snowman motif   Start here for scarf
End here for hat   Start here for hat

Row 3: K25, M1, K3, M1, K22.
Row 4: P to end.
Continue inc 1 st each side of gusset on next and every other row until there are 62 sts.
P 1 row.
Next row: K40, turn and cast on 2 sts.
Next row: P16, turn and cast on 2 sts: 18 sts.
Work 1" in st st on these 18 sts, ending with a P row.
Next row: K1, [K2, K2 tog] 4 times, K1: 14 sts.
Next row: P to end.
Next row: ✭ K2 tog, rep from ✭ to end, break off yarn, thread through sts, then draw up tightly and secure.
Join seam of thumb.
Return to remaining sts.
Join on yarn at base of thumb and with right-hand needle, pick up and K4 sts from base of thumb, K remaining 22 sts from left-hand needle: 52 sts.
Beg with a P row, work 1½" in st st, ending with a P row.
Shape top
Row 1: K2, [skpo, K19, K2 tog, K2] twice.
Row 2 and every other row: P to end.
Row 3: K2, [skpo, K17, K2 tog, K2] twice.
Row 5: K2, [skpo, K15, K2 tog, K2] twice.
Row 7: K2, [skpo, K13, K2 tog, K2] twice.
Row 9: K2, [skpo, K11, K2 tog, K2] twice: 32 sts.
Bind off.

TO FINISH
Duplicate stitch snowman motif on back of mitten, then embroider as for hat. Join top and side seam.

LEFT MITTEN
Work as for right mitten from ✭ to ✭.
Shape thumb gusset
Row 1: K22, M1, K1, M1, K25.
Row 2: P to end.
Row 3: K22, M1, K3, M1, K25.
Row 4: P to end.
Continue inc 1 st each side of gusset on next and every other row until there are 62 sts.
P 1 row.
Next row: K36, turn and cast on 2 sts.
Next row: P16, turn and cast on 2 sts: 18 sts.
Work 1" in st st on these 18 sts, ending with a P row.
Complete as for thumb of right mitten.
Return to remaining sts.
Join on yarn at base of thumb and with right-hand needle, pick up and K4 sts from base of thumb, K remaining 26 sts from left-hand needle: 52 sts.
Now complete as for right mitten.

INSTRUCTIONS FOR BABY'S MITTS
(make two)
Using smallest needles and A, cast on 38 sts.
K 15 rows. Work in rib as follows:
Rib row 1: K2, ✭ P2, K2, rep from ✭ to end.

Rib row 2: K1, P1, K2, ✭ P2, K2, rep from ✭ to last 2 sts, P1, K1.
Rep these 2 rows 3 more times.
Change to largest needles.
Inc row: K6, ✭ M1, K5, rep from ✭ to last 2 sts, K2: 44 sts.
Beg with a P row, work in st st until mitt measures 4" from beg, ending with a P row.
Shape top
Row 1: K2, [skpo, K15, K2 tog, K2] twice: 40 sts.
Row 2 and every alternate row: P to end.
Row 3: K2, [skpo, K13, K2 tog, K2] twice: 36 sts.
Row 5: K2, [skpo, K11, K2 tog, K2] twice: 32 sts.
Row 7: K2, [skpo, K9, K2 tog, K2] twice: 28 sts.
Bind off.

TO FINISH
Duplicate stitch snowman motif on back of mitt, then embroider as for hat. Join top and side seam. Fold back cuff.

Make sure that your toddler's legs are warm in snowy weather by bridging the gap between boots and snowsuit with a pair of snug ankle-warmers.

CHRISTMAS STOCKING

A traditional Christmas stocking complete with fir trees and reindeer.

MATERIALS

6 oz (150 g) of a smooth medium-weight yarn, such as Patons Beehive D.K., in main color A.
2 oz (50g) of same in contrasting colors B and C
1 oz (25g) of a lightweight glitter yarn, such as Twilleys Goldfingering, in contrasting color D (used double)
A set of four size 5 and size 7 double-pointed knitting needles

GAUGE

24 sts and 30 rows to 4" measured over st st worked on smaller needles

To save time, take time to check gauge.

INSTRUCTIONS

Using smaller needles and A, cast on 72 sts and arrange over 3 needles, so placing 24 sts on each needle. Knit 36 rounds.
Next round (picot edge): ✳ yo, skpo, rep from ✳ to end
Knit another 40 rounds.
Using the larger needles for the Fair Isle rows and the smaller needles for the st st rows, work in pat from chart rep the 24 st-pat 3 times in each round, until row 59 has been completed.
Change to smaller needles. Knit 2 rounds.
Shape ankle
Next round: K1, skpo, K to last 3 sts, K2 tog, K1.
Knit 4 rounds.
Rep these last 5 rounds until 58 sts remain.
Shape heel
Break off A. Rearrange sts as follows:
Slip last 15 sts of third needle and first 16 of first needle onto fourth needle. (There should now be 31 sts on this needle.)
Divide remaining 27 sts onto remaining 2 needles and leave.
Join on C and work backward and forward in rows on 31 sts of first needle only, as follows:
Row 1: K to end.
Row 2: P to end.
Dec 1 st at beg of next 22 rows: 9 sts.
Now inc 1 st at end of next 22 rows by picking up corresponding decreased loop of previous 22 rows: 31 sts.
Break off C.
Join on A, and working in rounds over all 58 sts, knit 1 round, rearranging sts so that there are 20 sts on first needle and 19 on each of second and third and noting that round now begins at side edge of foot.

Knit 36 rounds. Break off A.
Join on C and knit 6 rounds.
Shape toe
Round 1: [K1, skpo, K23, K2 tog, K1] twice.
Round 2: K to end.
Round 3: [K1, skpo, K21, K2 tog, K1] twice.
Round 4: K to end.
Continue dec in this way on every other round until 22 sts remain. Bind off.

TO FINISH

Turn stocking inside out and join toe seam. Fold hem at top of stocking to wrong side and slipstitch in place. Using either crochet, braiding, or tubular knitting (see page 88), make a length of cord 8" long and sew to back at top edge of stocking.

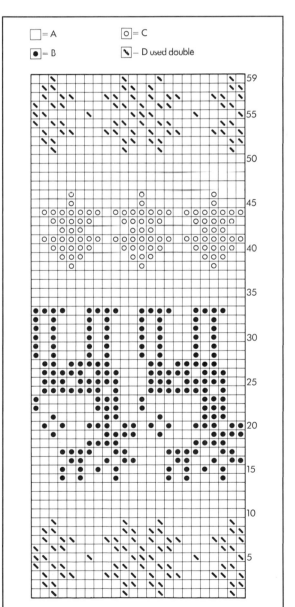

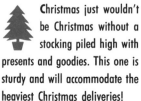 Christmas just wouldn't be Christmas without a stocking piled high with presents and goodies. This one is sturdy and will accommodate the heaviest Christmas deliveries!

AND SO TO BED

A luxurious little raglan-sleeved robe with a roll-over collar, deep pocket, and long tie belt.

MEASUREMENTS
To fit 22" chest
Actual measurement 32"
Length from shoulder 22"
Sleeve seam with cuff turned back 9"

MATERIALS
25oz (700g) of a cotton-blend bouclé yarn, such as Phildar Skate
A pair of size 8 knitting needles
A size H crochet hook

GAUGE
17 sts and 24 rows to 4" measured over pattern using yarn double

To save time, take time to check gauge.

NOTE

Yarn is used double throughout.

INSTRUCTIONS

BACK

Using yarn double, cast on 73 sts. K 3 rows.
Work in pat as follows:
Row 1 (right side): K1, * P1, K1, rep from * to end.
Row 2: P1, * K1, P1, rep from * to end.
Rows 3 and 4: K to end.
These 4 rows form the pat.
Continue in pat until back measures 15" from beg, ending with row 2 of pat.
Shape raglan
Bind off 4 sts at beg of next 2 rows.
Next row: K1, skpo, pat to last 3 sts, K2 tog, K1.
Next row: P2, pat to last 2 sts, P2.
Rep these 2 rows until 21 sts remain, ending with a wrong-side row. Bind off.

LEFT FRONT

* Using yarn double, cast on 47 sts. K 3 rows. *
Work in pat as follows:
Row 1: * K1, P1, rep from * to last 3 sts, K3.
Row 2: K2, P1, * K1, P1, rep from * to end.
Rows 3 and 4: K to end.
These 4 rows form the pat.
Continue in pat until front measures same as back to beg of raglan shaping, ending with a wrong-side row.
Shape raglan
Bind off 4 sts at beg of next row.
Pat 1 row.
Next row: K1, skpo, pat to end.
Next row: Pat to last 2 sts, P2.
Rep these 2 rows until 21 sts remain, ending with a wrong-side row.
Now work collar as follows:
Row 1: K4, * K1, P1, rep from * to last 3 sts, K3.
Row 2: K2, P1, * K1, P1, rep from * to last 4 sts, K4.
Rows 3 and 4: K to end.
Row 5: As row 1.
Row 6: K2, P1, * K1, P1, rep from * to last 4 sts, turn.
Row 7: Sl 1, K to end.
Row 8: K across all sts.
Rep these 8 rows until shorter edge measures 4".
Bind off.

RIGHT FRONT

Work as for left front from * to * .
Work in pat as follows:
Row 1: K3, * P1, K1, rep from * to end.
Row 2: * P1, K1, rep from * to last 3 sts, P1, K2.
Rows 3 and 4: K to end.
These 4 rows form the pat.
Continue in pat until front measures same as back to armholes, ending with a right-side row.

Shape raglan
Bind off 4 sts at beg of next row.
Next row: Pat to last 3 sts, K2 tog, K1.
Next row: P2, pat to end.
Rep these 2 rows until 21 sts remain, ending with a wrong-side row.
Now work collar as follows:
Row 1: K3, * P1, K1, rep from * to last 4 sts, K4.
Row 2: K4, * P1, K1, rep from * to last 3 sts, P1, K2.
Rows 3 and 4: K to end.
Rows 5 and 6: As rows 1 and 2.
Row 7: K to last 4 sts, turn.
Row 8: Sl 1, K to end.
Rep these 8 rows until shorter edge measures 4".
Bind off.

SLEEVES

Using yarn double, cast on 41 sts.
Work in pat as for back for 2" to form cuff.
Continue in pat increasing and working into pat 1 st each end of next and every following 6th row until there are 57 sts.
Work straight until sleeve measures 10½" from beg, ending with row 2 of pat.
Bind off 4 sts at beg of next 2 rows.
Shape raglan as for back until 5 sts remain, ending with a wrong-side row.
Bind off.

POCKET

Using yarn double, cast on 19 sts.
Rep the 4 pat rows 4 times, then rows 3 and 4 again.
Bind off.

BELT

Using yarn double, cast on 9 sts.
K 3 rows.
Work in pat as follows:
Row 1: K3, P1, K1, P1, K3.
Row 2: K2, [P1, K1] twice, P1, K2.
Rows 3 and 4: K to end.
Rep these 4 rows until belt measures approximately 52" or desired length.
Bind off.

BELT LOOPS (make 2)

Using crochet hook and with yarn double, make 14 ch, then fasten off.

TO FINISH

Block the work; do not press. Join raglan seams. Join center back collar seam, then sew edge of collar to sleeve tops and back neck. Join side and sleeve seams. Sew on pocket. Sew one belt loop to each side seam. Thread belt through loops.

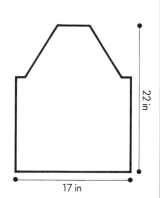

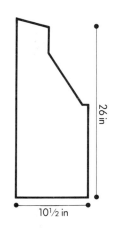

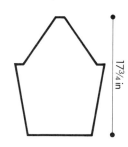

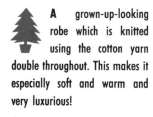 **A** grown-up-looking robe which is knitted using the cotton yarn double throughout. This makes it especially soft and warm and very luxurious!

SNOWFLAKES

This long-sleeved snowy sweater sports a Fair Isle design. It also has a slash neck and fastens with two buttons on each shoulder.

MEASUREMENTS

To fit 18(20,22)" chest
Actual measurements 22(24,26)"
Length from shoulder 11¼(12,13)"
Sleeve seam 8(9,10)"

MATERIALS

6oz (150g) of a smooth lightweight yarn, such as Pingouin Pingofine, in main color A
2oz (50g) of same in contrasting color B
A pair each of size 1 and size 2 knitting needles
4 buttons

GAUGE

32 sts and 40 rows to 4" measured over st st worked on larger needles
32 sts and 36 rows to 4" measured over Fair Isle pattern worked on larger needles

To save time, take time to check gauge.

INSTRUCTIONS

BACK AND FRONT (alike)

Using smaller needles and A, cast on 87(95,103) sts.
Rib row 1: K2, ✶ P1, K1, rep from ✶ to last st, K1.
Rib row 2: K1, ✶ P1, K1, rep from ✶ to end.
Rep these 2 rows for 1".
Change to larger needles.
Inc row: K12(16,20), ✶ inc in next st, K20, rep from ✶ to last 12(16,20) sts, inc in next st, K to end: 91(99,107) sts. Beg with a P row, work 3 rows st st.
Joining in B as required, continue in pat as follows:
Row 1: K1A, ✶ 1B, 3A, rep from ✶ to last 2 sts, K1B, 1A.
Row 2: P with A.
Row 3: K with A.
Rows 4 and 5: As rows 2 and 3.
Row 6: P3A, ✶ 1B, 3A, rep from ✶ to end.
Row 7: K with A.
Row 8: P with A.
Row 9: As row 7.
Row 10: As row 8.
These 10 rows form Dot pat.
Continue in pat until work measures approximately 6(6¾,7¾)" from beg, ending with row 10 of pat.
Now work from chart, working edge sts as indicated until row 44 has been completed.
Using A only, work 2 rows st st.
Change to smaller needles.
Rep the 2 rib rows 4 times.
Bind off.

SLEEVES

Using smaller needles and A, cast on 49(57,57) sts.
Work 1½" in rib as for back.
Change to larger needles.
For 1st and 2nd sizes only
Inc row: K10(14), ✶ inc in next st, K9, rep from ✶ to last 9(13) sts, inc in next st, K to end: 53(61) sts.
All sizes
Beg with a P(K,K) row, work 1(2,2) rows st st.
Increasing 1 st each end of next row, work 2 rows st st: 55(63,59) sts.
Now working in Dot pat as for back and front, inc and work into pat 1 st each end of 3rd and every following 4th row until there are 83(91,91) sts.
Continuing in pat, work straight until sleeve measures approximately 7¼(8½,9½)" from beg, ending with row 10 of pat.
Now work in pat as for first 6 rows of chart.
Bind off.

TO FINISH

Press or block as appropriate for yarn used.
Join shoulder seams for approximately 1".
Sew in sleeves, then join side and sleeve seams.
Make 2 button loops on each side of neck on front neck.
Sew buttons on back neck edge opposite loops.

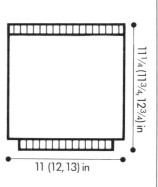

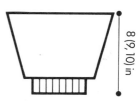

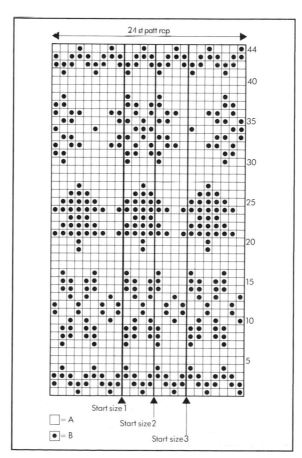

 This winter sweater has a band of Fair Isle pattern over the chest and shoulders and a flurry of snowflakes over the body and arms.

KNITTING KNOW-HOW

MATERIALS AND EQUIPMENT

The materials and equipment required for hand-knitting are generally inexpensive and lightweight – which is why knitters so often take their knitting around with them. The following is a list of the basics you are likely to need:

Knitting needles are the principal tool for hand-knitting. There are basically three kinds: single-pointed, circular, and double-pointed. Single-pointed needles are sold in pairs and come in lengths ranging from 10" to 16". They are sized from 0 to 15; the higher the number, the larger the needle. Metric-sized needles are used in Europe and are sometimes seen in the United States. Most knitting needles are made of metal or plastic, but you will also find them made of wood, bamboo, and ivory. The size of the needles required varies with the thickness of the yarn and the finished effect that the knitter desires. The smaller the needle, the tighter the knitting, and the larger the needle the looser is the work. When experimenting with your own designs it is not necessary to confine yourself to the size of needle recommended for the chosen yarn, for exciting textures can be created by deviating from these sizes.

The choice of lengths of needle should be made according to the number of stitches in the work and whatever feels the most comfortable for the knitter. They should be carefully stored in a dry, clean place so they do not become bent. Straight, clean needles facilitate even and fast knitting.

Circular needles are made with pointed plastic or coated metal sections on both ends of a flexible nylon section. They range in length from 16" to 40" and are specially designed for knitting in the round. When choosing a circular needle for this purpose, make sure that its length from point to point is at least 2" less than the circumference of the knitting, so that the fabric will not be stretched. You can also use a circular needle for knitting in rows, simply moving the fabric one end to the other.

Double-pointed needles have points at both ends and are used usually in sets of four. They are used for tubular knitting in items such as socks and neckbands which are too small for a circular needle.

A large tapestry needle is used for seams. It has a large eye at one end for ease of threading yarns and a blunt end to avoid splitting the yarn in the knitted pieces.

Stitch holders are often used in the shaping of necklines. When it is necessary to reserve some stitches from the body or the sleeves of the work, they are placed on a stitch holder until knitted into the main garment.

Needle gauges are usually plastic or metal frames with graduated holes which indicate the correct size of knitting needles.

READING KNITTING PATTERNS

CHOOSING THE YARN

Make sure the yarn you choose can be knitted up to the same gauge as that of the pattern. Check the label, or buy a sample ball and knit a gauge swatch. When buying yarn for a garment make sure that the whole quantity is from the same dye lot. Check the labels carefully, since they will state both the color number and dye lot number. Each dye lot differs in shade fractionally and there could be a marked line on the garment where the balls of different dye lots have been joined.

GAUGE

The success of every knitted garment depends on using the correct gauge, and you will never become a competent knitter until you automatically check this every time you begin a new piece of knitting. Gauge refers to the number of stitches and rows over a given measurement, which is necessary to make the garment to the size as designed.

However experienced a knitter you are, it is essential to work a gauge swatch in the stated yarn before beginning a pattern. Then at this stage you can assess if any adjustments need to be made in needle sizes or in the design – before it is too late. The garment will turn out to be the correct size only if your gauge is exactly the same as the one stated on the pattern.

Before starting a pattern, knit a gauge swatch in the stated yarn and with the recommended needle size. Cast on a few more stitches than the figure given for the stitch gauge and work a few more rows than the figure given for the row gauge. Make sure that you also knit in the stated stitch pattern.

When you have worked a square, lay it on a flat surface and mark off the stated number of stitches and rows with pins. Do not start right at the edge stitch for these measurements. Now measure the distance between the pins. If you have too many stitches for the measurement, this means that your gauge is too small, and you should rework the square using a size larger needle. On the other hand, if there are too few stitches, your gauge is too large, and a size smaller needle should be used to rework the square. It is necessary to continue experimenting with different needle sizes until the correct gauge is achieved. You should also check the row gauge at

Needle sizes

US	Metric (approximate equivalents)
0	2mm
1	2¼mm
2	2¾mm / 3mm
3	3¼mm
4 / 5	3¾mm
6	4mm
7	4½mm
8	5mm
9	5½mm
10	6mm
10½	6½mm / 7mm
11	8mm
13	9mm
15	10mm

the same time, but it is easier to add a few rows to the depth of a garment, keeping the stitch pattern correct, than it is to adjust the width of a garment. Another advantage of working a gauge swatch is that it enables you to gain some experience with the stitch pattern used in your garment. It will speed up your work when you begin, because you will be able to understand the terminology being used.

THE INSTRUCTIONS

After you have chosen the yarn and needles and worked a gauge swatch, it is time to begin the pattern. You will have already read the pattern with great care and marked the appropriate size you will be working. The pattern will indicate in which order the pieces are to be worked, and even though the choice may not be your own preference, it is advisable to stick to the order as printed. It is not uncommon to find instructions that relate to previously completed pieces for some necessary measurement. It is also advisable to join the pieces together in the order suggested, because this may be relevant for some further work, such as neckbands or collars.

Try to make a habit of checking your work as you go along, especially if it is a complicated and repeated stitch pattern. It is often easier for the eye to pick up a mistake during the course of a pattern than when the piece is completed. A careful check of the number of stitches is another indication that all is going according to plan. When you are checking the measurements of a piece of knitting, do so on a flat surface and with a rigid measuring tape. Do not measure around curved edges, but place your tape measure at right-angles to a straight edge of the rows.

Where graphs or stitch diagrams are used, remember that they only show the right side of the work and that each graph square represents one stitch. Therefore, the odd-numbered rows, or front side, should be worked from right to left, and the even-numbered rows, or reverse side, should be worked from left to right. For left-handed knitters the patterns should be read in the reverse direction. When knitting on circular needles, begin each round on the right-hand edge of each chart. Graphs are particularly popular for Fair Isle knitting and in collage or picture sweaters.

Another useful hint is to remember never to leave your knitting in the middle of a row; if you have to leave the knitting for any length of time do not leave it in the middle of a piece. You will discover, when you recommence, an ugly ridge across the row where you stopped knitting, and it is virtually impossible to remove it.

When knitting in rows, try, wherever possible, to join new balls in at the end of a row, since a knot in the middle of a row of knitting will result in an unsightly hole. If it is unavoidable to have a mid-row join, as when knitting using circular needles, join yarns by splicing the ends together as described on page 133.

ABBREVIATIONS

The accompanying list of abbreviations needs to be studied carefully to enable you to use the section of knitting patterns. In some of the patterns there are extra abbreviations that are relevant only to that particular pattern; in such cases these are explained at the beginning of the pattern.

K	knit
P	purl
st(s)	stitch(es)
st st	stockinette stitch (1 row K, 1 row P)
rev st st	reverse stockinette stitch (1 row P, 1 row K)
pat	pattern
rep	repeat
beg	beginning
inc	increas(ing)
dec	decrease(ing)
oz	ounces
g	grams
g st	garter stitch (every row K)
sl	slip
tog	together
psso	pass slipped stitch over
skpo	slip 1, knit 1, pass slipped stitch over
tbl	through back of loop(s)
yo	yarn over
yfwd	bring yarn forward
ybk	bring yarn back
pw	purlwise
kw	knitwise
M1	Make one, worked as follows: pick up strand between stitch just worked and next stitch on left-hand needle and knit into back of it.
sl 1 pw	slip one purlwise
ch	chain
sc	single crochet

BASIC SKILLS

Before attempting to knit any garment, it is necessary to master a few basic knitting techniques and stitches. It is advisable to practice with a spare ball of yarn until you can knit with an even tension to produce a smooth fabric. Then you can confidently embark on a pattern.

The basics of learning to knit are very simple – casting on, binding off, increasing and decreasing, and the two elementary stitches of knit and purl. Most patterns consist of differing combinations of these two stitches.

One of the commonest methods of casting on is the cable, or two-needle method shown here. Binding off – always done with two needles – may be done on a knit or a purl row, or even in a ribbed pattern.

CASTING ON

1. Make a slip loop (leaving a short length of yarn for finishing) and place it on the left-hand needle. Insert the right-hand needle through the loop on the left-hand needle, from front to back. Holding the yarn at the back of the needles, pass it under and over the point of the right-hand needle.

2. Draw the loop through the stitch on the left-hand needle to the front of the work and place it on the left-hand needle.

3. Insert the right-hand needle between the first two stitches, pass yarn under and over as before, draw yarn through and put it on the left-hand needle.

4. Continue making stitches in this way until the correct number have been cast on to the left-hand needle.

THE KNIT STITCH

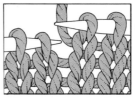

1. Hold the needle with the stitches to be knitted in the left hand with the yarn at the back of the work.

2. Insert the right-hand needle, front to back, through the first stitch; take the yarn under and over this needle.

3. Pull the new loop on the right-hand needle through the work to the front and slip original stitch off the left-hand needle.

Beginning a new row
When the end of the first row is reached, all the stitches are on the right-hand needle. Transfer this needle to the left hand, ready to begin the second row, and use the empty needle to knit with in the right hand.

THE PURL STITCH

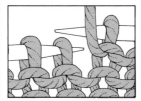

1. Hold the stitches to be purled in the left hand with the yarn at the front of the work.

2. Insert the right-hand needle, back to front, through the first stitch; pass the yarn over and around this needle from right to left.

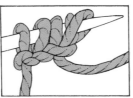

3 .Pull the new loop through the stitch and slip it off the left-hand needle. The new stitch remains on the right-hand needle.

Changing from knit to purl
After completing the knit stitch, bring the yarn through to the front of the work between the needles. Then purl the next stitch in the usual way.

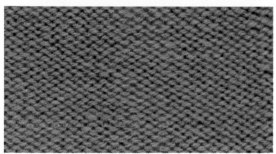

Top is a photograph of stockinette stitch seen from the front of the work. One row is knitted and the next is purled alternately. The right side is smooth and the back is ridged, as shown in the lower photograph.

When this side of stockinette stitch is used as the right side of the work, it is known as reverse stockinette stitch. When every row is knitted (or purled) this produces the stitch known as garter stitch.

THE SEED STITCH

This stitch – also sometimes called moss stitch – is one of the more basic stitches and is often used to fill in between pattern panels or as a border. The first row is worked by alternately knitting one stitch then purling the next. On the next row, if the first stitch facing you is a knit stitch (the smooth side of the stitch), it is worked as a purl stitch. If it is a purl stitch facing you (with the ridge standing out from the knitting), it is worked as a knit stitch.
All following rows are worked in this way, making sure that the stitches form the alternating knit and purl pattern going up as well as across the rows.

JOINING YARN

It is best to try not to run out of yarn in the middle of a row, for the joining knot will be evident from the front of the work. If it is unavoidable, use the following method to join the yarn. Unravel short ends of the two pieces of yarn, and overlap half the strands from each piece. Twist them together firmly. Cut the remaining threads. The method is known as "splicing" the yarn.

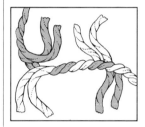

PICKING UP DROPPED STITCHES

When a dropped stitch occurs, a little patience will overcome the problem. It is not necessay to pull out the needle and undo several rows. Picking up is easily done on a simple stitch pattern, but much more difficult in the course of a complicated pattern. In this case it is preferable to unravel; but after you have rectified the problem, check that the number of stitches is correct before continuing with the work. To pick up a dropped stitch the only equipment you need is a crochet hook.

Picking up a knit stitch

Picking up a purl stitch

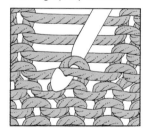

With the right side facing, insert the hook through dropped stitch from front to back. Place the hook around the strand immediately above the dropped stitch and pull the strand through the stitch. Repeat until the same level is reached as the rest of the work, and place the stitch on the left-hand needle.

With the wrong side facing, put the hook through the dropped stitch from back to front. Place the hook around the strand immediately in front and draw it through the dropped stitch. Repeat until the same level is reached as the rest of the work, and place the stitch on the left-hand needle.

UNPICKING MISTAKES

In the course of intricate pattern work, occasionally the number of stitches may vary from the original number. It is necessary to keep a careful check on the number of stitches so as not to throw out the whole pattern.

When a mistake is discovered, careful unpicking is the best way to rectify the error. If this is done stitch by stitch, taking care not to twist the stitches, no evidence of the unpicking will remain.

Unpicking knit stitches

Put left-hand needle through lower stitch. Pull right-hand needle out of the stitch above it and pull the yarn out with the right hand.

Unpicking purl stitches

With yarn at front on purl side, put left-hand needle in lower stitch, pull right-hand needle out of the stitch above and pull out yarn.

BINDING OFF

Follow the pattern as to which of three methods should be used for binding off. If no indication is given, bind off knitwise. Take care to bind off smoothly and fairly loosely; if the work is too tight the edge will pucker. On most neck edges it is advisable to bind off with a right-hand needle that is one size larger than those used for working the neckband. This will give the neckline more elasticity.

Binding off knitwise

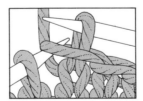

Knit the first two stitches. Insert the left-hand needle into the front of the first stitch, lift it over second stitch and off the

needle. Knit another stitch and repeat process until one stitch remains. Break the yarn and draw it firmly through the last stitch.

Binding off purlwise and in rib

To bind off purlwise, purl the first two stitches, and lift the first stitch over the second and off the needle. Continue purling and binding off to the last stitch and fasten off as above. For a ribbed bind-off (i.e. over a K1, P1 rib), as used on most neck and

armhole bands, knit the first stitch, then purl the second. Lift the first stitch over the second and off the needle. Knit the third stitch and lift the second over. Continue in this way until all the stitches are bound off. Fasten off the last stitch with the end of the yarn.

SHAPING

Nearly every knitted garment includes some shaping, either for sleeves or necklines, or in the basic body shape. Shaping is done either by increasing or decreasing stitches or by a combination of both. Where the object is solely to shape a garment, these techniques can be worked almost invisibly. However, they can also be used in a decorative way to create lacy and embossed stitch patterns.

DECREASING

This is the main method used to reduce the width of garments, especially for sleeve top and armhole shaping, and at a neckline. It is also the basis for many intricate but decorative stitch patterns. Always use the decreasing method that is given in the pattern. If no method is given, then use the "knit (or purl) two together" method.

Knitting two stitches together

Put the right-hand needle into front of second stitch and then front of first stitch, knitwise. Yarn around

needle, pull it through both stitches, then slip both stitches off left-hand needle.

Purling two stitches together

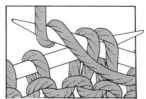

With yarn at front, insert right-hand needle into the front of the first and then the second stitch, purlwise. Wind the yarn

around the needle, and pull it through both the stitches, then drop them both off the left-hand needle.

Slipstitch decreasing, knitwise

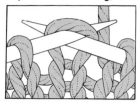
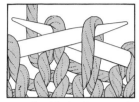

With the yarn at the back of the work, slip the first stitch from the left- to the right-hand needle, knitwise. Do not knit it. Now knit the second stitch. With the left-hand

needle, lift the first stitch over the second knitted stitch and off the needle. In patterns this is called "slip 1, knit 1, pass slip stitch over", abbreviated "sl 1, K1, psso" or skpo.

INCREASING STITCHES

The other commonly used method of shaping knitted garments is by increasing the number of stitches. This is also used extensively in intricate pattern designs, especially for lacy stitches. There are several methods of increasing stitches, some invisible and some decorative.

Invisible increasing

This is the simplest method of increasing. It is generally used to change the shape of a garment at the sides, but can be worked anywhere along a row just as successfully.

Two stitches from one knitwise

Knit into the front of the next stitch with the right-hand needle, but do not slip it off the left-hand needle. Now knit into the

back of the same stitch with right-hand needle, and slip the stitch off left-hand needle, making two from one.

Two stitches from one purlwise

Purl into the front of next stitch but do not slip it off the left-hand needle. With right-hand needle

purl into the back of this stitch again and then slip it off the left-hand needle.

Knitting into running strand between, knitwise

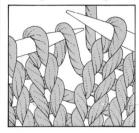

With the left-hand needle pick up the strand lying in front of it and keep the loop formed on the left-hand needle.

Knit into the back of this loop.

Slip it off the left-hand needle. This method is sometimes called "make one".

Knitting into running strand between, purlwise

With the left-hand needle pick up the loop lying in front of it and keep the loop formed on the left-hand needle.

Purl into the back of this loop.

Slip it off the left-hand needle.

Decorative increasing

In some patterns the increased stitch features as a decorative item, by creating a small hole with every increased stitch. The increased stitch is formed between two existing stitches by looping the yarn over the needle and is called a "yarn over."

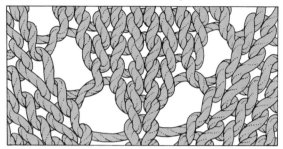

Yarn over, between two knit stitches

To make a new stitch between two knit stitches, bring the yarn under, then over, the right-hand needle.

Insert the needle knitwise into the next stitch and knit a new stitch as usual. The extra loop remains on the needle.

On the next row, if working stockinette stitch, purl into this new loop as usual.

Yarn over, between two purl stitches

To make a new stitch between two purl stitches, loop the yarn over, then under, the right-hand needle, so that it is again at the front of the work. Purl the stitch as usual. The extra

loop remains on the needle. On the next row, if working stockinette stitch, knit into the new loop as usual. If you are working a yarn-over between a knit and a purl stitch, or vice versa,

the movement will vary slightly, but still consists essentially of taking the yarn over the needle and into the correct position for knitting or purling, as the case may be.

ADVANCED TECHNIQUES

The following techniques require a little more skill than those alrady covered, but they are not difficult to acquire, for they incorporate the basic stitches that have alrady been learned.

Simple bobbles and cables are the basic design elements of many complicated patterns, but in themselves they are not difficult to master.

You will also need to learn multicolor techniques, even if you only want to use one additional color. Next come instructions for making buttonholes, for these are invariably found on cardigans, jackets and vests.

Lastly, it is also necessary to learn how to pick up stitches along the edges of knitting in order to form collars and armholes.

CABLE

All forms of cable are worked on the principle of moving a number of stitches from one place to another in the same row. Up to two stitches at a time can be moved quite easily, using only two knitting needles, but when it is necessary to transfer more than this number, it is easier to use a short, double-pointed cable needle. The stitches to be moved are held on the cable needle, at either the front or the back of the work, until needed.

Simple cable knitwise

Take the right-hand needle around the back of the first stitch on the left-hand needle, and knit into the back of the

second stitch. Then knit into the front of the first stitch and slip both stitches off the left-hand needle together.

Simple cable purlwise

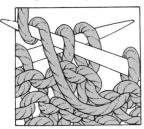  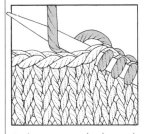

Take the right-hand needle in front of the first stitch on the left-hand needle and purl into the front of the second stitch.

Then purl into the front of the first stitch and slip both stitches off the left-hand needle at the same time.

Cabling with a cable needle

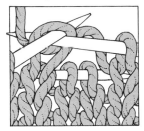

Cable twist to right: slip two stitches onto a cable needle and put it at the back of the work. Knit

Cable twist to left: slip two stitches onto a cable needle and put it at the front of the work. Knit the next two stitches, then knit the two stitches from the cable needle.

the next two stitches and then knit the two stitches from the cable needle.

BOBBLES

The principle of making bobbles is always to make more than one stitch from the stitch where the bobble is desired and then decrease back to the original stitch in the same or a later row.

To make a bobble

Knit to the position where the bobble is required. Make five stitches from the next stitch by knitting into the front then back of the stitch twice, and then knit into the front again. Turn and purl these five stitches, turn and knit the five stitches. With the left-hand needle lift the second, third, fourth and fifth stitches over the first stitch and off the right-hand needle. Knit to position of next bobble and repeat.

PICKING UP STITCHES

Picking up on the bound off edge
Insert the right-hand needle through the first edge stitch. Take the yarn under and over the needle and make a knit stitch. Continue making knit stitches until you have the right number.

Picking up on the selvage
Working with the right-hand needle, put it through the fabric between the first two rows and form a knit stitch. Continue making knit stitches between every two rows.

BUTTONHOLES

Many patterns require buttonholes. The two main types are horizontal and vertical buttonholes, used on the bands of jackets and cardigans. When small buttonholes are needed, such as on lightweight clothing, simple eyelet holes are ideal, since they are neat and unobtrusive.

Horizontal buttonholes

Knit to the position of the buttonhole and bind off the required number of stitches to fit the button size. Continue to the end of the row. On the next row, work to the stitch before the binding off, knit into it twice, and then cast on one fewer number of stitches than were bound off on the row before. Continue working until the position of the next buttonhole is reached, and then repeat the process.

Vertical buttonholes

Knit to the position of the buttonhole and then divide the work and knit each side separately. When each side is long enough to fit the button comfortably, continue to work across the whole row. Continue working until the position of the next buttonhole is reached, and then repeat the whole process.

Eyelet buttonholes

See next page.

To make eyelet buttonholes

Work to the position of the buttonhole. Bring the yarn forward between the needles to the front of the work and take it over the needle to knit the next two stitches together.

On the next row, purl the yarn taken over. To make a channel for threading ribbon or cord, work a succession of eyelets across the row at the point where a channel is required.

BUTTON LOOPS

These loops are one of the simpler methods of placing buttonholes on a knitted garment.

Start by threading a needle with yarn in the appropriate colour, then join the yarn to the edge of the garment, in the position for the button loop, by taking a few small stitches.

Take the needle a little farther along the edge, just under the width of the button, and make a small stitch, leaving a loop large enough to go over the button. Insert the needle back through the fabric at the original place and take another small stitch. Repeat so that there are three thicknesses of yarn for the loop.

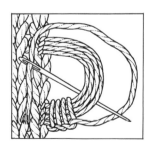

Finishing off

Neatly work buttonhole stitch over all of the threads to cover the loop completely.

MULTICOLOR PATTERNS

Modern hand-knitting uses a great deal of multicolor work, either to emphasize a pattern or in careful blending of colours, and in collage and graph knitting.

Different kinds of multicolor pattern require different techniques. In Fair Isle knitting, which uses two colors in any one row, the two methods used are stranding and weaving. Although it may at first appear difficult to handle two or more balls of yarn at the same time, once these techniques have been mastered, the problem quickly disappears.

Stranding is usually used if the pattern is small with only three or four stitches work in each color. If there are more than five successive stitches in one color, it is better to use the weaving technique, so that long loops are not left on the back of the knitting.

Joining in new colors

Colors can be joined in at the beginning of or during a row of knitting. This needs to be done smoothly and securely, so that no holes result where there is a join, especially in the middle of a knitted piece.

At the beginning of a row

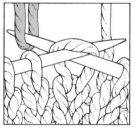 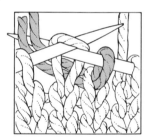

Insert the right-hand needle into the first stitch, and with the first color make a loop; then make

one with the new color over this needle. Finish the stitch by pulling these loops through in the normal way. To make more secure, work the next two stitches with both ends of the new yarn. At the end of the next row be careful to treat the last three stitches as single stitches.

In the middle of a row

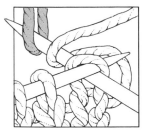

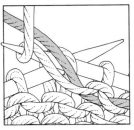

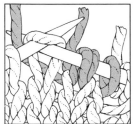

Knit to the position where the new color is to be introduced. Insert

Stranding colors

After joining in the new color in one of the above methods work with the

Weaving colors knitwise

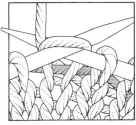

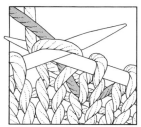

When the contrasting yarn is carried across more than five stitches it must be woven into the back of the work. Keep first color in the right hand and second in the left. Knit the first stitch in the usual way, but on the

right-hand needle into the next stitch, and with the new color make a loop around the end of this needle. Make the stitch in the normal way, but work the next two stitches with both ends of the new yarn. When working the next row remember to treat these as single stitches.

first color and loosely carry the new yarn across the back of the work until it is needed. Change to the new color and strand the first color across the back until it is needed once more.

second and every other stitch put the right-hand needle into the stitch, loop the left-hand yarn across top of the needle, then work the stitch in the normal way with the first color.

Weaving colors purlwise

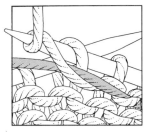

On the purl side, weave the colors alternately over and under on every stitch. Weave it over by inserting the needle into the next stitch, pass the yarn to be woven over the top of the needle, then purl the stitch with

first color in the normal way. On the next stitch weave the yarn under the stitch by keeping the woven yarn pulled taut with the left hand while purling the stitch in the normal way with the first color.

DUPLICATE STITCH

Also called Swiss darning, this is a simple technique, using a contrasting yarn to embroider the surface of stockinette stitch by imitating and covering each knitted stitch with the contrasting yarn. Provided it is worked carefully, without pulling the yarn too tightly, it is almost impossible to tell that it has not been knitted by using the motif knitting technique. Whenever contrasting motifs are used within knitting, it is nearly almost possible to work the whole section of knitting in one colour only, then to duplicate stitch the motifs before finishing.

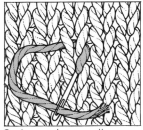

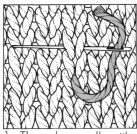

1. Thread a needle with contrasting yarn and fasten at back of work. Bring needle through to front of work, through the center of the stitch below the stitch to be covered. Insert the needle through the knitted fabric, under the stitch in the row above, and draw the yarn gently through.

2. Insert the needle back through the fabric at the base of the embroidered stitch. Repeat steps 1 and 2 as necessary to form the motif.

WORKING FROM CHARTS

Normally a chart is given in a knitting pattern when it would be too complicated to give out the pattern row by row. Sometimes a chart is given to show where different stitch patterns must be worked, but usually they are used for color patterns and motifs which are worked in stockinette stitch. On the chart each square represents one stitch to be knitted and one row to be worked.

If the design is an all-over pattern, the yarn not in use can generally be stranded or woven in across the back of the work, but if there are large areas of one color use a separate ball of yarn for each block of color.

To prevent holes in the work join each section of color together by twisting the yarns together on the wrong side of the work every time you change color.

On a knit row

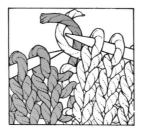

Knit in first yarn to position for changing color. Keeping yarns at back of work, place the first color over the second color, then pick up the second color and knit to the next color change.

On a purl row

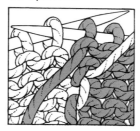

On a purl row, work as for a knit row, but keep yarns at front of work. Always twisting yarns together, as on a knit row, when changing color.

FINISHING

The loose ends of yarn, at either side of the knitting, should be darned into the back of the work. Then trim the yarn close to the fabric.

Most pieces of knitting require either blocking or pressing before they are sewn together. This will bring the work to the correct shape and smooth out minor irregularities in the knitting.

To block, first cover a flat surface, such as a board, with a folded Turkish towel. Place the work, right side up, on the towel and pin it out to the correct measurements, using rustproof pins and placing them about 1" apart. Do *not* include the ribbing. Spray the work evenly, or lay a wet press cloth on top, and leave it to dry thoroughly.

If pressing is required (for example, on stockinette stitch knitted in wool or cotton), use a press cloth and apply the iron gently, in an up-and-down movement; do not slide it or let its weight rest on the work. Never press a textured stitch pattern.

SEWING UP

Follow the pattern carefully as to the order in which the pieces should be sewn together, as this may be relevant to any further work, such as neckbands or collars. The two main methods of joining the edges are an invisible seam or a backstitch seam.

The latter is the stronger seam and is best when working against the grain of the fabric. When sleeves are sewn in, the stitches should not be so tight that there is no room for stretching.

Invisible seam

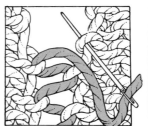

Lay the two sections flat, right side upward and edges matching. Secure the yarn at a lower corner. The needle must be passed under the strand between the first two edge stitches. Now pick up the next strand on the opposite side and firmly draw the two edges together, without any puckering. Continue along the length of seam.

Backstitch seam

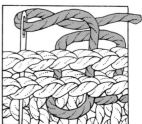

Place right sides together, matching the edges. Secure yarn at bottom. Work from right to left over one knitted stitch at a time. To begin, take yarn across one stitch at back and through to front. Take yarn back to the right by one stitch through to back, to the left by two stitches and to the front. Continue till complete.

GRAFTING

An alternative method to binding off and then sewing edges, such as the shoulder seams, together, is to graft them. In order to do this, you leave the stitches that would otherwise be bound off, on a spare needle or holder until the pattern tells you to join that seam.

A grafted seam is ideal for baby clothes, because besides being totally invisible, it has no hard ridges which result when two edges are sewn together.

To Work the Grafted Seam

Leave the stitches that are to be joined on a holder or a spare length of yarn until needed.

Place the two pieces to be joined on a flat surface, with the knitted side upward and with the two sets of stitches opposite each other.

Thread a needle with a length of yarn approximately four times the length of the seam.

Fasten the yarn to one edge and bring the needle up through the first stitch on one of the pieces of knitting.

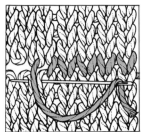

Take the needle across to the other set of stitches and up through the first stitch, then back to the first set of stitches and down into the first stitch. Then take it up through the second stitch on that side, then across to the other side and down into the first stitch. Then take it up through the second stitch, then back down into the second stitch on the first side. Continue until the end is reached. Fasten off securely.

POMPONS

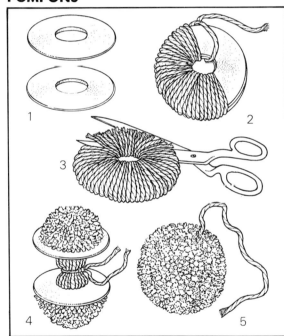

1. Cut two circles of cardboard to the diameter required for the pompom. Cut a smaller circle out of the center of each one, about a third of the total diameter.
2. Holding the two rings together, wind the yarn around and around the rings until the center hole is almost filled.
3. Inserting the blade of the scissors between the edges of the two rings, cut through the yarn around the edge.
4. Gently pull the rings apart; using an extra piece of yarn, tie it tightly around the center of the pompom and fasten off securely.
5. Pull the cardboard rings off the pompom, and fluff up into shape.

AFTER-CARE

Washing Always use warm, never hot, water and a washing detergent specially manufactured for cleaning knitwear. Do not soak hand-knitted garments, and avoid the need for this with frequent and brief washes. When the garment is wet, never lift it by the shoulders, as it is very easy for the weight to distort the shape. If you live in a hard-water area, add fabric conditioner to the last rinse, so that the natural pile of the yarn is released. Rinse then gently squeeze out the excess water.

Drying This should be done on a flat surface, away from direct heat and sunlight. Ideally, place the wet garment on a newspaper that has been covered by a thick, clean towel. Pat out any creases and leave until dry. You may want to give the garment a few minutes in a tumble drier to fluff it up a little. Mohair and angora sweaters often benefit from being left overnight in the refrigerator in a plastic bag.

Pressing If the washing and drying have been carried out carefully, pressing should not be necessary. If it is still thought desirable, check the yarn label for the correct temperature setting for the iron, and follow the same instructions for pressing as given for finishing in the pattern or on the yarn label.

Wear and tear The two most common signs of wear and tear are small balls of fiber forming on the surface of a garment and snagging. The small balls can be removed with a specially designed comb which can be bought from a notions department or with manicure scissors. To remove snags use a tapestry needle, and pull the snag through to the reverse side. Gently adjust the stitch to its original shape and size and knot the end at the back.

LAUNDRY SYMBOLS

Yarns manufactured in Europe bear symbols, on their labels, indicating the recommended care of garments made with them. The washtub indicates suitability for washing and the correct water temperatures. The upper figure indicates the automatic washing cycle that is suitable for machine-washable yarns. The lower figure indicates the water temperature for hand washing. If the yarn is suitable only for hand washing a hand will be shown in the tub, and if the tub is crossed through, the yarn is then suitable only for dry cleaning. When bleach can be used a triangle with the letters CL inside will appear, but generally the triangle will be crossed out, since most yarns cannot be bleached. Suitable ironing temperatures are shown by an iron containing three dots for hot, two for warm, or one for cool. An iron crossed out indicates that pressing is not recommended.

Extreme care should be given to a garment knitted with a mixture of yarns, and the lowest temperature shown on the label should be used.

For dry cleaning a circle appears with the letters A, P or F, which refer to the different dry cleaning solvents. A crossed-out circle indicates that the garment cannot be dry cleaned.

YARN MANUFACTURERS, AGENTS AND RETAILERS

Anny Blatt

Laines Anny Blatt
24770 Crestview Court
Farmington Hills
Michigan 48018

Berger Du Nord

Brookman & Son Ltd
4416 NE 11th Avenue
Fort Lauderdale
Florida 33334

Canada
Berger du Nord
9697 St Laurent
Montreal
Quebec N3L 2N1

Emu

Plymouth Yarn Co Inc
PO BOX 28
500 Lafayette Street
Bristol
PA 19007

Jaeger

Susan Bates Inc
212 Middlesex Avenue
Route 9A
Chester
Connecticut 06412

Canada
Patons & Baldwins
(Canada) Ltd
1001 Rose Lawn Avenue
Toronto
Ontario

Patons

(as Jaeger)

Phildar

Phildar Inc
6438 Dawson Boulevard
Norcross
Georgia 30093

Canada
Phildar Ltee
6200 Est
Bd H Bourassa
Montreal Nord H1G 5X3

Pingouin

Pingouin Corporation
PO Box 100
Highway 45
Jamestown
South Carolina 29453

Canada
Promafil Canada Ltd
300 Boulevard Laurentien
Suite 100
St Lauren
Quebec H4M 2L4

Rowan

Westminster Trading
Corporation
5 Northern Boulevard
Amherst
New Hampshire 03031

Canada
Estelle
39 Continental Place
Scarborough
Ontario M1R 2T4

Sirdar

Kendex Corporation
31332 Via Colinas, No 107
Westlake Village
California 91362

Canada
Diamond Yard
153 Bridgeland Avenue
Unit 11
Toronto
Ontario M6A 2Y6

Twilleys

Rainbow Gallery
13615 Victory Boulevard
Suite 245 Van Nuys
California 91401

Gemini
720 East Jericho Turnpike
Huntington Station
New York 11746

YarnWorks

Tanglewool
57 Church Street
Lenox
MA 01240

Coulter Studio
118E Square Street
NY 10022

The Knitting Basket
5812 Grove Avenue
Richmond
Virginia 23226

If you have difficulty obtaining
any of the yarns recommended
in this book, you can write to
the companies listed here for
information on retailers and
mail-order services.

ACKNOWLEDGEMENTS

Editor Isabel Papadakis
Art Editor/Design Pat Sumner
Assisted by Brazzle Atkins
Production Controller Maryann Rogers
Pattern Editor Sue Hopper

Photography Fiona Alison
Styling Amanda Cooke, Hilary Guy, Vicky Wood
Illustrations Jeremy Firth, Coral Mula, Lindsay Blow

The publishers would like to thank the following for supplying clothes and props for photography:
Benetton (0–12)
H and M Hennes
Klimages
Lott 32, Camden, NW1
The London Toy and Model Museum
The Pet Shop, Harlsden, NW10
The Pine Mine, Wandsworth, SW6
Ravel
Rosemary Smith, handmade buttons on pages 18, 37, 70 and 129
Villeroy and Boch

The Teddy Bears photographed are British made by Merrythought and are available from most good toy shops and department stores.

The verse on page 98 is from 'Furry Bear', *Now We are Six*, by A.A. Milne, Methuen Paperbacks.

The Publishers would also like to thank Tessa for all her hard work and productivity, the additional designers, and all the knitters including Mrs Edna Booth, Mrs Margaret Burgess, Mrs Vera Jones and, in particular, Mrs Gina Watts-Russell.